NEW ZEALAND
Woman's Weekly

OUR QUEEN

Jenny Lynch

50 YEARS SINCE THE CORONATION

RANDOM HOUSE
NEW ZEALAND

A RANDOM HOUSE BOOK
published by
Random House New Zealand
18 Poland Road, Glenfield,
Auckland, New Zealand

www.randomhouse.co.nz

First published 2003
© New Zealand Magazines
© Photographs New Zealand Magazines and holders as specified on page 112

The moral rights of the author have been asserted.

ISBN 1 86941 569 8

The Publisher wishes to acknowledge Jennifer Wieland, Paula Maihi, Angie Harrison and Louise
Richardson from New Zealand Magazines, and Margaret McCloy for their help with photo research.
Special thanks also to the many editorial, photographic, administrative and production staff of the
New Zealand Woman's Weekly through the years whose work made a book like this possible.

Picture research: Terry Snow and Nicola McCloy
Cover, text design and layout: Trevor Newman, Auckland
Printed by: Hutcheson, Bowman and Stewart, Wellington

National Library of New Zealand
Cataloguing-in-Publication Data

Lynch, Jenny (Jennifer Ann)
Our Queen : 50 years since the coronation / Jenny Lynch.
ISBN 1-86941-569-8
1. Elizabeth II, Queen of Great Britain, 1926-
2. Queens—Great Britain—Biography. I. Title.
941.085092—dc 21

Contents

Chapter One

A HEAVY CROWN

IT HAD BEEN ALMOST 16 MONTHS SINCE 27-YEAR-OLD ELIZABETH HAD ASCENDED THE THRONE ON THE DEATH OF HER FATHER KING GEORGE VI.

W hat were the occupant's thoughts as she took in the cheers of her flag-waving subjects? In the early years of her reign the Queen was reportedly a great worrier. And although she appeared perfectly composed – she had been well-schooled in self-control – it would have been strange indeed had she not experienced the faint fluttering of butterfly wings on this, her day of days.

Certainly, she had no need to fear the coronation procedure. She knew exactly what was expected of her, for the various rituals had been thoroughly rehearsed both at Buckingham Palace and the Abbey itself. Initially, Elizabeth had prepared alone, reading and memorising large portions of the rite. She had walked around the white drawing room with a length of fabric pinned to her shoulders to represent her heavy ceremonial train, and balanced books on her head to get the feel of the crown the Archbishop of Canterbury would place on her head.

That crown. It was a whopper. Made in 1661 for Charles II of solid gold and encrusted with pearls, rubies, diamonds, sapphires and emeralds, the St Edward's Crown weighed 2.25 kg – about the same as an extra-large size 22 frozen chicken.

Queen Victoria declined to wear it at her coronation; the lighter Imperial Crown of State, made specially for the occasion, served instead.

Edward VII followed his mother's lead and it had been suggested that Elizabeth do likewise. But she refused. St Edward's was the official crown and the massive St Edward's she would endure.

RIGHT: SPLENDOUR. OFFICIAL PORTRAIT OF THE NEWLY crowned Elizabeth II in Westminster Abbey with two of the symbols of her office. In one hand she carries the Orb and in the other the Sceptre with the Cross.

BELOW: BELOVED KING. THE DEATH OF KING George VI in 1952 came as a shock to Britain and the Commonwealth. But, as the *Weekly* reported, 'in the midst of their grief the loyal subjects of the Crown could find it in their hearts to rejoice for the new sovereign and acclaim the reign of the second Elizabeth'.

With every move planned and practised down to the last inch, it was unlikely the Queen would falter. But what if someone else did? During the homage to Queen Victoria a 'dreadfully infirm' peer had toppled over and rolled down the steps, while an elderly cleric had fainted and held up the works at her father's coronation. The anointing could pose problems. Elizabeth I had complained that the sacred oil was 'nasty grease and smelled ill'. While the preparation with which the second Elizabeth would be anointed was unlikely to cause offence – it had been made to a perfumed formula close to the one Charles I had devised for his coronation – much depended on the firmness of the hand that delivered it to the royal forehead. At the coronation of the Queen's great-grandparents Edward VII and Queen Alexandra, the aged archbishop had managed to overdo things and a trickle of oil had run down Alexandra's nose.

ABOVE: CROWNING. THE ARCHBISHOP OF CANTERBURY, Dr Geoffrey Fisher, raises the heavy St Edward's Crown high in the air before placing it on Elizabeth's head. While usually seen as the climax, the crowning is only a small part of the coronation ceremonial which includes the Recognition, Oath, Anointing, Investiture, Homage and Communion.

ABOVE: WEIGHTY RESPONSIBILITY. SEATED IN THE high-backed oak chair built for King Edward I, Elizabeth carries the Sceptre with the Dove (symbolising justice and mercy) in her right hand and the Sceptre with the Cross (symbolising her temporal power as ruler) in her left. At 10 kg, the Coronation Robes – made of gold thread for King George IV – are so heavy that tiny 19-year-old Queen Victoria was unable to wear them at her coronation. But Elizabeth opted for all the Regalia.

ABOVE: HEAVY CROWN. DOUBTLESS ELIZABETH WAS relieved that she did not have to wear the St Edward's Crown for long. It weighs about the same as an extra-large size 22 frozen chicken. By the time she left the Abbey the St Edward's had been replaced by the much lighter Imperial State Crown.

PROCESSION. ESCORTED BY THE GENTLEMEN-AT-ARMS, THE QUEEN WALKS THROUGH the Nave to the West Door of Westminster Abbey after the end of the three-hour service. Her four attendants carry the crimson ermine-trimmed ceremonial train.

In Queen Alexandra's day there was no television. Only those closest to her had observed her anguish. Now for the first time the coronation would be televised. Any slight slip or mishap and the world – well, those with television sets – would see. The decision to allow BBC cameras into Westminster Abbey had been controversial. Prime Minister Winston Churchill, the archbishop and the Queen's private secretary Tommy Lascelles had been set against the idea, fearing that telephoto lenses would explode the mystique and mystery of the monarchy. The prospect of people watching proceedings in inappropriate venues such as pubs further appalled the august trio. But, just as she had over the question of St Edward's crown, Elizabeth put her foot down. She believed that her coronation should be seen and enjoyed by as many people as possible. And if that meant television, so be it.

What else might have been on the Queen's mind as she made her way to the Abbey? Her children. Earlier, as her coach rolled through the gates of Buckingham Palace, it had been watched from an upstairs window by four-year-old Prince Charles and his sister Anne, aged two. Charles would later be driven through back streets to the Abbey to join his grandmother and Aunt Margaret in the Royal Gallery. What if the little prince got all excited and cried out, 'There's my mummy!'?

ABOVE: SOUVENIR MUGS. THE CORONATION OF QUEEN ELIZABETH II was seen as the birth of a glorious new Elizabethan era. And doubtless many among the three quarters of a million people who cheered the young sovereign to and from the Abbey invested in tangible reminders of the grand occasion.

LEFT: SOUVENIR COVER. MEMORIES OF THE CORONATION WILL have been fresh in New Zealanders' minds as they prepared to welcome the Queen to this country – the first visit by a reigning sovereign – at the end of 1953. So it wasn't surprising that the *Weekly* of 24 December featured a coronation cover.

ABOVE: FAIRY TALE. IT LOOKS LIKE THE KIND OF coach in which Cinderella might have travelled to the ball. The magnificent gold State Coach – built in 1761 for George III – which carried the Queen and Prince Philip to and from the Abbey had onlookers gasping in appreciation and delight.

BELOW: SOUVENIR. NEW ZEALANDERS WERE ALSO able to obtain programmes of the coronation service. The elaborately designed programmes, issued by King George's Jubilee Trust, were distributed throughout the United Kingdom and the Commonwealth.

ABOVE: TV BAN. BRITISH PRIME MINISTER WINSTON Churchill, seen here with the Queen, Princess Anne and Prince Charles, tried to halt planned BBC television coverage of the coronation, believing that intrusive cameras would place too much of a strain on the Queen. Palace officials – described by one newspaper as a bunch of codheads – feared also that close-ups might threaten the mystique of the monarchy. But in the end Elizabeth's wishes were what counted, and she wanted as many people as possible to see the service. The BBC went ahead and the coronation became the first televised royal spectacular.

PUBLISHED BY GRACIOUS PERMISSION OF HER MAJESTY THE QUEEN

THE CORONATION OF HER MAJESTY QUEEN ELIZABETH II APPROVED SOUVENIR PROGRAMME

KING GEORGE'S JUBILEE TRUST

The day itself was going to be a long one. There is no record of what shoes the Queen wore beneath her white satin Norman Hartnell-designed gown. Presumably they were comfortable ones. Six hours would pass between Elizabeth's arrival at Westminster Abbey at 11 a.m. and her appearance, together with other members of the royal family, on the balcony of Buckingham Palace in the late afternoon to acknowledge applause from the sea of well-wishers below.

The St Edward's Crown, doddery participants, the holy oil, television, little Prince Charles, tired feet – all may have fleetingly engaged the Queen's attention. But it is certain that her thoughts went first and foremost to the enormity of the sacred trust she would shortly take on as she accepted the symbols of her office – the Spurs, the Sword of State, the Armills, the Orb, the Ring and Glove, the Sceptre and the Rod.

To her subjects she represented the promise of a glorious new Elizabethan age. They expected their Queen to live up to that promise. They expected her to be perfect.

The *Weekly* wrote: 'The young Queen will . . . hold in her hands the destiny of a nation who have come, through the wisdom and goodness of her illustrious forebears, to place their faith in the Crown.'

In her Christmas broadcast the previous December, Elizabeth had asked people to pray on coronation day that she be granted the wisdom and strength to carry out the solemn vows she would make.

The years ahead would see the Queen encountering adulation that sometimes bordered on hysteria. (During her 1953-54 New Zealand visit, reporters went into raptures over 'her exquisite complexion, her eyes like sapphires and her beautiful mobile mouth as she talked and smiled'.) But they would bring carping criticism, too. Also danger. Sadness. And shocking family troubles.

In due course Queen Elizabeth II would need every one of those coronation day prayers.

RIGHT: CORONATION STUNNER. THE QUEEN WANTED her coronation dress to be designed along the lines of her wedding gown. Royal couturier Norman Hartnell obliged with an opulent white satin creation embroidered with emblems of Britain and the Commonwealth in diamonds, pearls, amethysts and gold thread. This portrait of Elizabeth wearing the gown was published two days after coronation day.

ABOVE: POSTAL TRIBUTE. SIGNIFICANT ROYAL events call for special stamps and the coronation issue depicted the Queen with the Orb, Sceptres and the floral emblems of Great Britain. British people writing to Antipodean friends and relations could also do so on specially designed aerogrammes featuring coronation themes.

LEFT: EXCITED CHILDREN. FOUR-YEAR-OLD Prince Charles was taken to the Abbey to see his mother crowned but two-year-old Princess Anne (apparently much to her annoyance) remained at Buckingham Palace where she watched proceedings on television. Later, however, both children were able to join their parents on the palace balcony to acknowledge rapturous applause from the huge crowds below.

RIGHT: CORONATION ROUTE. The 8.3-km route from the Abbey back to Buckingham Palace was designed to provide as many people as possible with a glimpse of the newly crowned Elizabeth. The procession itself was 3.2 km long and the Queen took one hour and 40 minutes to complete the journey.

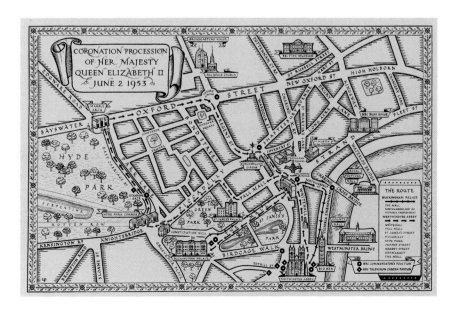

LEFT: GREAT OMEN. HOW APT THAT news of Edmund Hillary's conquest of Mt Everest reached the British public on the morning of coronation day. The New Zealand climber was part of a British team led by Colonel John Hunt and, accompanied by Sherpa Tenzing Norgay, reached the top of the world's highest mountain at 11.30 a.m. on 29 May.

OPPOSITE PAGE: ADULATION. New Zealanders got their chance to see the newly crowned Queen during her 1953-54 visit and the *Weekly* marvelled that she was 'so much more beautiful than her photographs'. On one occasion we described Elizabeth as 'truly quite lovely', on another as 'sweet and girlish', and we were enchanted by her 'exquisite complexion' and 'eyes like sapphires'. The Queen is pictured here with the Duke of Edinburgh at the start of their Greymouth-Christchurch train journey leg of the tour.

ABOVE: TWO ORBS. MOST pictures of the Queen at her coronation show her holding the Orb. This 1 kg hollow gold ball is the emblem of sovereignty and dates from Charles II's time. The smaller Orb pictured at left was made for Queen Mary, the wife of William of Orange. William and Mary were joint rulers and, as a sovereign in her own right, Mary was thus entitled to her own Orb.

EARLIER CORONATIONS

The 20th century saw four other sovereigns take the throne. Edward VII's coronation had to be postponed when he underwent an operation for appendicitis. It finally took place in shortened version a fortnight later on 9 August 1902 with nurses in attendance to provide help if needed.

George V and Queen Mary endured seven hours of ceremonials on 23 June 1911; and in 1937 George VI took over the coronation on 12 May originally intended for his older brother Edward VIII who had earlier abdicated.

According to tradition, the Queen Dowager does not attend the coronation of a new sovereign. However, Queen Mary felt that, given the special circumstances of George VI's coronation, a display of royal solidarity was required. The gesture was evidently much appreciated, for it was reported that during the procession to the Abbey, the cheers for Mary - who shared a carriage with the Princesses Elizabeth and Margaret - were sometimes louder than those for the King and Queen.

Chapter Two

FAIRYTALE PRINCESS

WHEN THE DUKE AND DUCHESS OF YORK WELCOMED ELIZABETH ALEXANDRA MARY INTO THE WORLD ON 21 APRIL 1926, THEY HAD NO IDEA THEY WERE PRESENTING BRITAIN AND THE COMMONWEALTH WITH THEIR FUTURE QUEEN. WHY WOULD THEY?

After all, Elizabeth was only third in line to the throne. Her father's older brother Edward, known as David in the family, was the one who (barring untimely death) would eventually step into King George V's shoes. While David as yet demonstrated none of the sterling qualities needed for kingship – he appeared largely devoted to fun, frivolity and dalliances with married women – duty decreed that he would one day settle down with a partner from the admittedly diminishing pool of European princesses and produce his own successor.

So Elizabeth's early years were light-hearted ones free from any shadow of responsibility. It was an idyllic time – weekdays in London; weekends at the Royal Lodge at Windsor Great Park; summer holidays at Glamis Castle, the Scottish home of her maternal grandparents. The little Princess did not want for toys. (The Duke and Duchess returned from their 1927 tour of Australia and New Zealand laden down with three tons of dolls, teddy bears and other nursery paraphernalia.) Or for pets – Elizabeth got her first pony at the age of three. At first nothing too arduous on the learning front interfered with daily pleasures. Governess Marion Crawford, known as Crawfie, took care of the educational basics. Later, Margaret Rose, born in 1930, joined her sister in the oak-panelled schoolroom of 175 Piccadilly.

ABOVE: 'WE FOUR'. THAT'S HOW KING GEORGE VI described his close-knit family in the early years of his reign. The King and Queen attempted to make the Princesses' upbringing as ordinary as possible and the huge hems on the girls' skirts (enabling the skirts to be let down as the wearers grew taller) indicate that Elizabeth and Margaret certainly received lessons in thrift.

LEFT: CORONATION OF GEORGE VI. LITTLE DID Princess Elizabeth suspect as she joined her parents and sister Margaret on the Buckingham Palace balcony on 12 May 1937 that one day it would be her turn to take centre stage as Britain's newly-crowned sovereign. The Princess was apparently worried that Margaret might not behave herself during the coronation service but later reported that 'I only had to nudge her once or twice.'

BELOW: EARLY START. PRINCESS ELIZABETH GOT HER first pony at the age of three and by her 13th birthday had become an accomplished rider.

ABOVE: FAIRY PRINCESSES. PRINCESS ELIZABETH, AGED nine, and five-year-old Margaret with their parents the Duke and Duchess of York in 1935. Elizabeth's early years were light-hearted ones with the educational basics supplied first by the Queen and then by Governess Crawfie (Marion Crawford). Crawfie later became persona non grata with the royal family when she spilled the beans about life with the Princesses.

LEFT: GIRL GUIDES. GUIDING WAS AMONG THE MANY recreational activities (others revolved around pets, amateur theatricals, parlour games and dressing up) enjoyed by the young Elizabeth and Margaret. The 34-strong Buckingham Palace Guide pack, with members from the children of court employees gave the sheltered Princesses a taste of the world of ordinary children.

BELOW: ROYAL BEAUTY. SHE WAS christened Margaret Rose and appears every inch an English rose in these delightful 1950 and 1958 studies. More outgoing than her serious-minded sister, Margaret as a child was also more difficult to discipline. The Princess's lesser status (of which she was keenly aware) led the King and Queen to indulge her by way of compensation, something they later may have regretted.

Both 'fairy princesses' were adored by their home-loving parents and enjoyed a closer relationship with them than was usual in upper-crust homes. Every morning after breakfast (when at home) the Duke and Duchess conducted prayers and father Bertie spoke fondly of his close-knit family as 'we four'.

But in January 1936 nine-year-old Elizabeth experienced the first of the changes that were to drastically affect her life. George V, her beloved 'Grandpa England', died. Because Uncle David, now Edward VIII, had yet to tie the marital knot and was consequently childless, this brought her one step closer to the throne.

She would soon move forward another step. Unbeknown to Princess Elizabeth a storm cloud had settled over the royal family. It took the form of a brash, bold and bossy divorcee called Wallis Warfield Simpson. David had fallen for Wallis in a big way. His shenanigans with the curiously unattractive American had already scandalised fellow family members. Now the new King wanted Wallis to share his throne. Constitutionally the idea was a non-starter. Edward had to choose: Wallis or the throne? He plumped for Wallis.

The abdication of 10 December catapulted the shy and diffident Bertie into the hot seat as George VI and Elizabeth became heir presumptive.

Woman's Weekly

RIGHT: ROYAL CHARMER. HE WAS HANDSOME AND personable but lacking in grit. And when it came to the crunch the Prince of Wales, later Edward VIII, felt unable to continue his duties as King 'without the help and support of the woman I love' – that woman being domineering divorcee Wallis Warfield Simpson. The Prince abdicated in 1936. This brought to an abrupt end the comparatively carefree life of the Duke and Duchess of York, pictured here in a New Zealand visit in 1927, and recast the future of 10-year-old Princess Elizabeth.

LEFT: LOVE AFFAIR. THE DUKE AND Duchess of Windsor pictured in France. Queen Elizabeth (the late Queen Mother) felt a deep resentment toward the former Wallis Warfield Simpson for stealing Edward VIII's heart and mind, thus causing him to turn his back on the throne. She believed that the stress her husband suffered as King contributed to his death at age 56. Wallis for her part loathed the Queen, whom she termed 'that fat Scotch cook' or 'Cookie'. She detected Elizabeth's influence behind King George's refusal to allow her to be titled Her Royal Highness.

RIGHT: RELUCTANT MONARCH. KING GEORGE VI receives the homage of a peer during his 1937 coronation. The new King, a shy, nervy man who was plagued by a stammer, felt ill-equipped for monarchical responsibility ('I had a sinking feeling inside') and was keenly aware of the changes it would bring to his family life.

In February of the following year the family moved from their comfortable Piccadilly home into Buckingham Palace.

Apart from the various discomforts of that 'draughty museum' (mice skittered behind the panelling and many rooms relied on a single electric bulb for light), life at first went on much as before for the Princess. While Elizabeth had to be prepared for her future role, her parents realised that this had to be sensitively handled with no sudden changes that might alarm and no spoiling that might lead to unattractive big-headedness. Previous sovereigns had made ghastly mistakes with their heirs. Edward VII had been educationally force-fed in a vain bid to bring him up to the required intellectual standard. He rebelled and ended up concentrating on one of the few things he did really well – womanising. The later Edward's upbringing failed to curb his hedonistic tendencies or instil a sense of responsibility. He became bored with his royal duties and at one point confessed that he was 'fed up with all this princing' and didn't want to be King anyway.

Until now Elizabeth's education had been along conventional lines with an emphasis on languages. But with ominous drum-beats sounding in Europe, history and current affairs would soon take on increasing importance.

Shortly after the outbreak of war both Princesses moved to Windsor Castle where they remained cloistered for the following two years, but as the threat of invasion lifted, Elizabeth was allowed to join activities, largely connected with charities and the war effort, designed to broaden her outlook, provide greater contact with the outside world and give her a taste of what she could expect as a fully fledged member of the 'family firm'.

Life nevertheless wasn't all work and no play. In March 1944 the *Weekly* reported that the 17-year-old Princess was helping entertain guests at Buckingham Palace and that the King and Queen had 'arranged several small, jolly dances for her'.

ABOVE: WAR EFFORT. KING GEORGE HAD BEEN RELUCTANT TO GRANT his elder daughter's request to join up in the services but Elizabeth's persistence finally wore him down. The 18-year-old Princess joined the Auxiliary Territorial Service at Aldershot where she learned how to strip and service an engine, and drive in convoy.

RIGHT: BELOVED FATHER. TWENTY-YEAR-OLD PRINCESS Elizabeth with George VI. The Princess idolised her 'papa' who in turn felt deeply protective toward her. He endeavoured to shield both his daughters from the prying press and for much of their childhood permitted only carefully posed pictures. Indeed, few things angered the King more – and he was given to sudden rages which his family termed 'gnashes' – than photographs of the snatched variety.

LEFT: FAMILY GROUP. THERE WAS NOTHING snatched about this 1951 family photograph. Top row: (from left) the Duke of Kent, Princess Margaret, Princess Alexandra, Marina, the Duchess of Kent, the Duke of Gloucester, Princess Elizabeth, the Duke of Edinburgh, the Duchess of Gloucester. Middle row: Queen Mary, King George holding Princess Anne, Prince Charles, Queen Elizabeth. In front: Prince Richard of Gloucester, Prince Michael of Kent, Prince William of Gloucester.

RIGHT: DANCING QUEEN. WELL, NOT QUITE. ELIZABETH was still a Princess when this photograph of her dancing an eightsome reel at the Royal Caledonian Hall in London appeared in the *Weekly.* Both she and Margaret enjoyed music and dancing and during the war took leading roles in Christmas pantomimes at Windsor.

BELOW: ROYAL HIDEAWAY. IN THE EARLY YEARS OF WORLD WAR II THE Princesses were said to have been spirited away to a place of safety 'somewhere in the country'. They were actually in Windsor Castle, 32 km from London, where they remained for the duration. The thought of Hitler imagining that they might be holed up in some remote village caused considerable merriment. Windsor – from which the royal family takes its surname – would later become the Queen's weekend home.

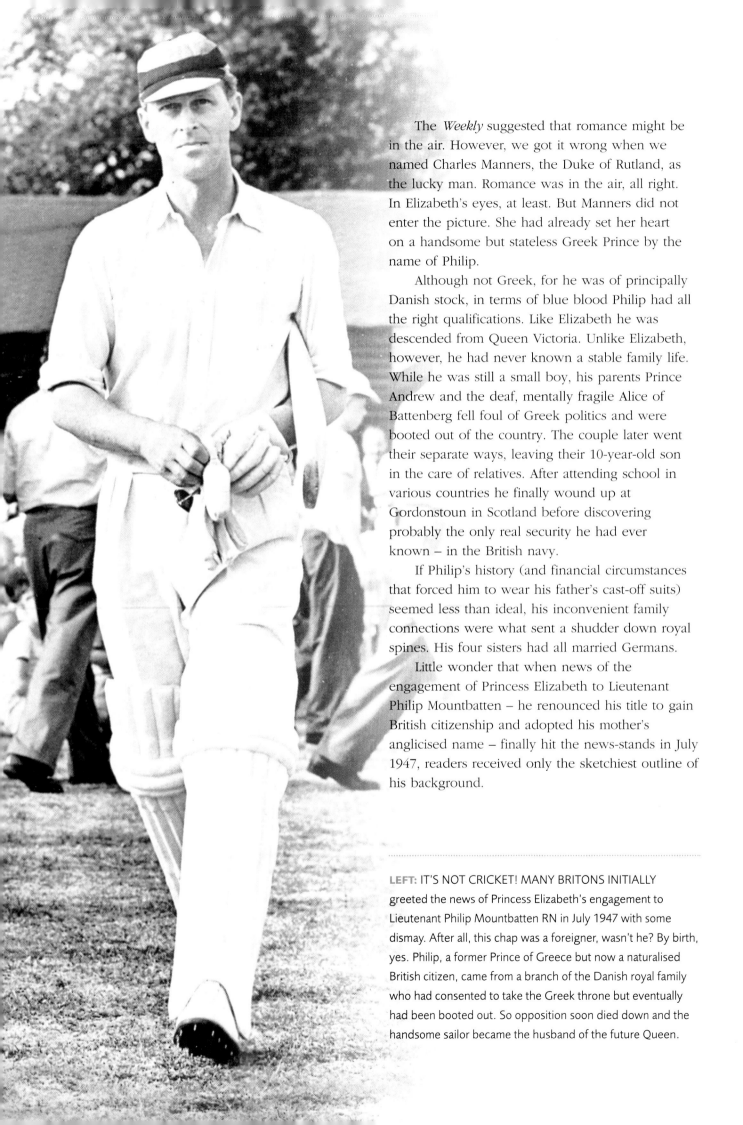

The *Weekly* suggested that romance might be in the air. However, we got it wrong when we named Charles Manners, the Duke of Rutland, as the lucky man. Romance was in the air, all right. In Elizabeth's eyes, at least. But Manners did not enter the picture. She had already set her heart on a handsome but stateless Greek Prince by the name of Philip.

Although not Greek, for he was of principally Danish stock, in terms of blue blood Philip had all the right qualifications. Like Elizabeth he was descended from Queen Victoria. Unlike Elizabeth, however, he had never known a stable family life. While he was still a small boy, his parents Prince Andrew and the deaf, mentally fragile Alice of Battenberg fell foul of Greek politics and were booted out of the country. The couple later went their separate ways, leaving their 10-year-old son in the care of relatives. After attending school in various countries he finally wound up at Gordonstoun in Scotland before discovering probably the only real security he had ever known – in the British navy.

If Philip's history (and financial circumstances that forced him to wear his father's cast-off suits) seemed less than ideal, his inconvenient family connections were what sent a shudder down royal spines. His four sisters had all married Germans.

Little wonder that when news of the engagement of Princess Elizabeth to Lieutenant Philip Mountbatten – he renounced his title to gain British citizenship and adopted his mother's anglicised name – finally hit the news-stands in July 1947, readers received only the sketchiest outline of his background.

LEFT: IT'S NOT CRICKET! MANY BRITONS INITIALLY greeted the news of Princess Elizabeth's engagement to Lieutenant Philip Mountbatten RN in July 1947 with some dismay. After all, this chap was a foreigner, wasn't he? By birth, yes. Philip, a former Prince of Greece but now a naturalised British citizen, came from a branch of the Danish royal family who had consented to take the Greek throne but eventually had been booted out. So opposition soon died down and the handsome sailor became the husband of the future Queen.

ABOVE: GOOD SHOT. PRINCESS ELIZABETH takes aim on board the HMS *Vanguard* in 1947 while on the way to South Africa where she toured with her parents and Margaret. King George had introduced his daughter to the art of rifle shooting two years earlier at Balmoral and Elizabeth managed to bring down a fine stag. Her skill at deer stalking later earned her a dressing-down from animal-rights campaigners.

LEFT: FAMOUS BROADCAST. WHILE IN South Africa with her family Elizabeth turned 21. To mark the occasion she made a speech from the grounds of Government House, Capetown, in which she pledged that her whole life 'whether it be long or short' would be devoted to the service of her future subjects.

Some grumbled, of course ('Not another foreigner!') but the splutterings soon died away. After all, Philip was such a good-looking chap. Manly, too – a far cry from some of the weedy wonders among the British aristocracy who might have attempted to win the pretty Princess's heart. Besides, everyone loves a royal wedding. And the union of fairytale princess and heartthrob prince was seen as just the thing to lift the gloom of post-war austerity.

Norman Hartnell designed an exquisite ivory satin wedding gown encrusted with crystals and 'pearls'. (A Golders Green chemist had manufactured 7000 of the latter with the aid of an essence made from fish scales.) Presents ranging from trousers and nylon stockings to mink coats poured in from around the world, and one brewery company instructed the managers of its hotels to shout their regular customers a drink in honour of the royal couple.

On the great day in November massive crowds lined the route to Westminster Abbey and Bob Hope, one of several Hollywood stars observing the wedding procession, declared that while Hollywood was accustomed to razzle-dazzle, 'I guess you have to come over here for real pageantry.'

In the Abbey Elizabeth promised to 'love, honour and obey' the newly created Duke of Edinburgh and later the 'sublimely happy' newlyweds, accompanied by Elizabeth's favourite corgi Susan, travelled by train to Uncle Dickie Mountbatten's Broadlands home in Hampshire for their honeymoon.

During the following four years Princess Elizabeth came as close as she ever would to leading the ordinary life of a naval wife. But that ended forever on 6 February 1952.

LEFT: BRIDE-TO-BE. THIS formal portrait issued shortly before the wedding depicts a serene and happy Princess. Elizabeth was never in any doubt that Philip was the one for her. She fell for him in her mid-teens and never wavered in her devotion.

LEFT: WEDDING DAY. KEEN observers noted that in the wedding photographs of Princess Elizabeth and the Duke of Edinburgh (he had received his new title a day earlier) the usual positions of bride and bridegroom were reversed. Elizabeth stood on her husband's right not, as some people supposed, because she feared that her gown might get tangled up in his sword but because she ranked above him in precedence. The *Weekly* noted: 'The only time the Duke of Edinburgh was on the right-hand side was when they were at the altar when – all being equal in the sight of God – precedence no longer held sway.'

RIGHT: POPULAR. THE RAPTUROUS RECEPTION GIVEN Princess Elizabeth and the Duke of Edinburgh during their Canadian tour at the end of 1951 probably helped take the princess's mind off worries over her father's health – the King had had an operation for the removal of his left lung and although appearing to have recovered well, the long-term prognosis was bleak. A jewel-laden Elizabeth is pictured responding in delight to something said during the state dinner at Government House, Ottawa.

Chapter Three

IN HARNESS

TO NEW ZEALANDERS NEWS OF KING GEORGE VI'S DEATH IN FEBRUARY 1952 CAME AS A DREADFUL SHOCK. CERTAINLY, HE HAD BEEN ILL. BUT ONLY THOSE CLOSEST TO HIM HAD KNOWN JUST HOW ILL. THEY ALONE HAD KNOWN THAT CANCER WOULD SHORTLY CLAIM HIS LIFE.

Yet when the King farewelled Elizabeth and Philip on 31 January on the start of a tour designed to bring them eventually to this country, he had seemed no more frail than usual. The Princess had no cause to suspect that within days her father would be dead.

While Britain and the Commonwealth grieved for the untimely loss of a monarch who had impressed with his decency and devotion to duty, however, there was, as the *Weekly* put it, 'no despair in their sorrow, but rather the bright spark of faith in the destiny held in the slim hands of a young Queen'.

For some it might seem, personal grief aside, that those 'slim hands' had inherited an enviable destiny. After all, Elizabeth would be the richest woman in the land. Her wealth would make a Lotto winner seem poor. She would be waited on hand and foot – a personal maid to dress her, chauffeurs to drive her about, chefs to attend to her culinary whims. There would be advisors to guide her on official matters and ladies-in-waiting to relieve her of less weighty tasks, like responding to letters from adoring fans. Add a handsome husband, two lovely youngsters (with nannies to take care of the less enchanting aspects of motherhood), several homes and a wardrobe to die for – what a life!

ABOVE: SERVICE AND SACRIFICE. DIAMOND EARRINGS and necklace, a gorgeous jewel-encrusted gown and that famous smile – the Queen at her most glamorous. But as her grandmother Queen Mary once remarked, being a sovereign is 'no bed of roses'. The *Weekly* wrote at the start of Elizabeth's reign: 'She has more love and probably more loneliness than any other woman in the world. As the first lady of the land there is no union to demand for her the blessings of a 40-hour week. Marriage has brought her two children whom she obviously adores, yet her position gives her less time with them than the humblest working mother enjoys.'

LEFT: SUPPORTING ROLE. THE DUKE OF EDINBURGH MAY initially have had difficulty adjusting to his second-fiddle role, but apart from the odd blunt comment that has got him into trouble, he soon learned to play it to perfection. During the 1963 tour, the *Weekly* raved about his 'lean and handsome face' and suggested that his ears must have burned as the compliments from girls floated to him from the crowds. Said one besotted teenager, 'For the Duke I'd give up Cliff Richard.'

ABOVE: FINAL FAREWELL. THE GUN CARRIAGE BEARING the coffin of King George VI travels through the streets of London toward St George's Chapel, Windsor, where the funeral service and interment took place. While Britain and the Commonwealth mourned the passing of the King, there was – as the *Weekly* put it – no 'despair in their sorrow', for in Elizabeth they had a sovereign fully worthy to take his place. 'The new Queen,' we said, 'commands respect for her qualities of dignity, virtue, honour, stability and sincerity – and affection for her gaiety of spirit and sense of fun.'

ABOVE: PARLIAMENT. THE QUEEN HAS PROBABLY LOST count of the times she has opened Parliament in Britain and various Commonwealth countries, but this occasion in 1952 is probably one she will always remember. A smiling Elizabeth, rugged up in luxurious furs against the November cold, leaves Buckingham Palace in the Irish Free State Coach for her first State Opening of Parliament.

Yes, but it would also be a life largely devoid of something most of us take for granted – spontaneity. From now on Elizabeth would be ruled by the calendar – Royal Maundy when coins are distributed to the poor just before Easter; Trooping the Colour and Royal Ascot in June; Balmoral in August; Christmas at Sandringham. She would also be ruled by the clock. No slacking off or sleeping in. A Queen can't afford to take a sickie. Not even when the royal yacht *Britannia*'s rocking and rolling delivered a nauseous blow to the stomach, as it once did when visiting the Channel Islands, could she afford to lie low. Elizabeth went ashore smiling rather than disappoint the waiting crowds.

Were the Queen to list the events of a typical working day in London during the early years of her reign it might have gone something like this: wake-up call at 7.45 a.m. (maid Bobo brings in cuppa); get dressed and breakfast with Philip; see children Charles and Anne at 9 a.m.; in the office at 10 a.m. for meeting with private secretary Tommy Lascelles to do business of the day and plan forward engagements; 11.30 a.m. receive ambassador; lunch; 1.30 p.m. attend to State papers; 3.30 p.m. open hospital memorial wing; back to palace by 5 p.m. for time with children and feet up.

Then, as now, Elizabeth evidently liked to avoid evening functions where possible. She preferred to leave cigar smoke-laden dinner gatherings to Philip. But Parliament openings, receptions for foreign Heads of State, the regular Tuesday meeting with the prime minister, investitures (the *Weekly* noted during one tour investiture that the Queen kept flexing her gloveless medal-pinning fingers as if in pain) and garden parties were among the many engagements for which rain checks were out of the question.

Overseas tours, however, have been the real test of Elizabeth's stamina and devotion to duty. During the monster six-month 1953-54 tour when

ABOVE: AT THE COALFACE. ROYAL DUTIES CAN TAKE A SOVEREIGN TO SOME UNLIKELY PLACES and July 1958 saw the Queen donning pit helmet, overalls and boots to go down the mine at Rothes Colliery, Kirkcaldy, in Scotland. She spent more than 40 minutes 500 m underground watching miners working different sections of the coalface, and saw the full mining cycle of cut, bore and strip.

ABOVE: SURPRISE. DURING THE 1970 NEW ZEALAND visit the Queen hit an informal note when, to the astonishment of the British press contingent ('it's never happened on a public occasion before') she wore slacks and a headscarf to a pageant at Ship Cove depicting the arrival of Captain Cook.

ABOVE: RACEDAY. ROYAL ASCOT IS AN ANNUAL JUNE event. On this particularly fine day in 1966 the Queen and Duke of Edinburgh were able to use an open carriage, pulled by four Windsor Greys, for the traditional royal drive up the course at the opening of the race meeting.

LEFT: COMMONWEALTH. A 1960S photograph at the Commonwealth Heads of Government conference in London. New Zealand Prime Minister Keith Holyoake is at left in the front row and the Queen is flanked by Canadian Prime Minister John Diefenbaker (left) and Robert Menzies of Australia. Whatever her personal views of the various Heads the Queen, who is apolitical, must keep them strictly to herself and be equally cordial to everyone. It is known, however, that she has found it easier to relate to some of her British prime ministers than to others. The relationship between the Queen and Margaret Thatcher is said to have been somewhat frosty.

RIGHT: PITCH, TOSS AND WALLOW. WHEN striking rough seas, the royal yacht Britannia – seen here off Picton in 1970 – could give its passengers some nasty moments. According to royal biographer Helen Cathcart, the Queen claims to have found her sea-legs as a horsewoman, 'and yet after sailing through a February storm she once wrote to a friend, "I was so miserable I would willingly have died".'

she attended 223 receptions and made more than 150 speeches, she lost so much weight that clothes started swimming on her and her maid had to make emergency alterations.

That particular tour, Elizabeth's first as sovereign, called for considerable preparation beforehand, for she had to familiarise herself with the customs of the 15 countries she would visit. It is unlikely that New Zealand threw up any nasty surprises, although Maori warriors advancing with bulging eyes and flicking tongues initially might have seemed alarming. It was probably just as well, however, that Philip warned her about kava's soapy taste so she could compose her features appropriately before downing the ceremonial beverage in Fiji.

Of course, the Queen is required to keep delivering her famous smile. Everyone expects it. Never mind the pompous officials, the boring speeches, the endless handshakes (4800 of them alone on the Australian leg of the 1953-54 tour), a

Queen must love every moment. ('She's not smiling – how awful, she doesn't like us!') She must also ignore discomfort. Those who planned her light summer wardrobe in 1963 had anticipated neither the Auckland drizzle – during her previous visit the deputy mayor had had to loan her his plastic raincoat – or the blustery Wellington winds.

Little wonder the Queen caught a mild cold. The *Weekly* asked: 'Couldn't somebody who understands the changeable New Zealand weather have passed on a word of advice? Several times at outdoor events she [must have] felt chilled to the marrow.'

Chills and officialdom aside, the Queen appeared to take genuine pleasure in her visits. It would have been a churlish monarch indeed who failed to respond to the enthusiasm with which she was welcomed by ordinary New Zealanders. Especially during the early tours, crowds went into raptures over their 'lovely, corker and fabulous' sovereign.

ABOVE: QUEEN'S BIRTHDAY. PEOPLE OFTEN WONDER why the Queen celebrates her birthday in June when she was actually born in April. The custom originated with Queen Victoria whose birthday fell in May. Because the Queen liked to spend that particular month at her 'dear Balmoral', it was decided to celebrate officially in June. Victoria's successor, Edward VII, had a November birthday – when Britain's weather is often at its worst – so he opted to retain the June celebration, and June it has been ever since.

ABOVE: YOUTH RALLY. THE QUEEN SMILES AS GLOVED hands reach out to her in the Auckland Domain while the Duke of Edinburgh eyes the marching girls. More than 16,000 children and their teachers (one for every 24 pupils) turned out in December 1953 for this meticulously organised event. The routes to water taps were carefully marked for the youngsters, and first-aid officers stood by to attend to any who might succumb to the heat and excitement. As royalty should never set eyes on anything as base as a public lavatory, the toilets were camouflaged behind palm fronds.

LEFT: GLOBE-TROTTER. THE Queen is the most-travelled sovereign in history and her State Visits have called for some unusual and sometimes uncomfortable modes of travel. In India in 1961 she found herself atop a gold-decorated elephant. On the same trip she endured miles and miles of bumpy roads 'always standing at the back of an open car, one hand grasping the rail of the seat in front of her . . . holding up her other arm, waving and smiling hour after hour'.

ABOVE: FLAG DUTY. THE QUEEN PRESENTS HER COLOUR to the RNZAF at Whenuapai, Auckland, in December 1953. The *Weekly* commented, 'A significant feature of the Queen's visit is the example she sets . . . steadfastness is her watchword . . . There is no complaint of strain or fatigue, no relaxation of interest, no abatement of cheerfulness as she performs the arduous duties relative to her heritage.'

ABOVE: CONVERSATION. ESCORTED BY THE PRIME Minister Keith Holyoake, Elizabeth chats with members of the official party on her arrival at Waitangi at celebrations to mark the 123rd anniversary of the signing of the Treaty of Waitangi in 1963. In the course of her travels the Queen meets hundreds of officials – some undoubtedly stiff and stuffy – but has a pleasant word for everyone and is said to be surprisingly easy to talk to. She has a marvellous memory and people who have met her once have sometimes been surprised on the second occasion to be addressed by name.

Weekly editor Jean Wishart wrote in 1963 of the thrill experienced by people who met the monarch. 'They recall the way she tosses back her head a little as she talks, how readily her eyes crinkle with laughter, and how unaffected her conversation is. Those who imagined that [the Queen] might rely almost entirely on questions ("What do you do? Where do you come from?") to get a conversation rolling were delighted to discover that she was willing to offer her own ideas and opinions.'

With so many children clambering to see her in 1963 – at Waitangi some young daredevils even shinned up a Norfolk pine for a better view – it must have been tempting for the Queen to talk about her own youngsters in far-off England. Leaving them behind had been a wrench and she missed them sorely.

Indeed, many of the Queen's greatest heartaches over the following years would centre on her family.

A speck of fluff on coronation day signalled the first crisis. At Westminster Abbey eagle-eyed reporters observed Princess Margaret flicking an offending thread from the RAF uniform jacket of the Queen Mother's comptroller, Group-Captain Peter Townsend. It was just a small gesture but an intimate one – and it spoke volumes. Who was this Townsend? Surely the pair couldn't be personally involved?

ABOVE: RAIN, RAIN, GO AWAY. BUT IT FAILED TO DO so during parts of the 1953-54 tour. The Queen carried her own umbrella (the Duke apparently braved the drizzle unprotected) because she'd found that when other people did the honours water sometimes ran down the back of her neck.

ABOVE: WINDY WELLINGTON. ENDURING DISCOMFORT with a smile. The *Weekly* felt that the Queen's advisors did her a disservice in 1963 for failing to consider New Zealand's changeable summer weather, particularly Wellington's blustery winds, when planning her light touring wardrobe. 'We could have saved her from including a sniffle among her souvenirs,' we said.

RIGHT: POI. THE ROYAL couple appeared delighted with the spectacular Maori songs and dances performed for them at Waitangi in 1963. The crowd 'roared its delight and clapped' when the Queen, who always tries to familiarise herself beforehand with the culture of countries she visits, uttered the words, 'Tena koutou katoa'.

BELOW: ACCOLADE. The Queen outside the Treaty House at Waitangi, accompanied by Sir James Henare. The 'breathtaking brilliance' of her peacock-blue raw silk outfit with matching hat met with onlookers' approval. 'Isn't she lovely!' people cried.

ABOVE: MAORI WELCOME. THE QUEEN MAY WELL have been a little taken aback by her first encounter with bulging eyes and flicking tongues in 1953, but by her second visit 10 years later she would have been better acquainted with the traditional challenge. During the 1963 visit she met a number of Maori dignitaries. Here Chief Te Kani Te Ua of Gisborne is presented to the royal couple at Waitangi.

They were. Heavily. The Queen already knew about it, and she was extremely concerned. She had always been close to her sister. She desperately wanted Margaret's happiness. And Margaret wanted to marry her lover.

In his autobiography *Time and Chance,* later serialised in the *Weekly,* Peter Townsend recalled 'the Queen's movingly simple and sympathetic acceptance of the extraordinary and disturbing fact of her sister's love for me'.

But what could she do? Townsend was divorced. The fact that he had been the innocent party made no difference. The Church of England did not condone divorce, and the Queen was the head of the Church. Elizabeth sought advice. Secretary Tommy Lascelles was unequivocal. He wanted to send the bounder packing.

Lascelles got his way. Townsend was posted to Brussels as air attaché on the assumption that by the time Princess Margaret turned 25 two years later and became free to marry without the Queen's consent, separation would have killed the controversial affair.

It didn't. However, Margaret's evident belief that she could now tie the knot with impunity was ill-founded. The government stepped in. Its message was clear. If she went ahead she would have to renounce all of her royal privileges.

'Frankly,' wrote Townsend, 'it would have ruined her.' Margaret bowed to the inevitable and doubtless the troubled Queen heaved a sign of relief.

But in years to come people would say: 'If only the Princess had been allowed to marry her one true love . . .'

ABOVE: DOOMED LOVE. MARGARET RETURNED Townsend's love and set her heart on marrying him, thus creating the first of many family crises in her sister's reign. The Queen wanted the 23-year-old Margaret to be happy but, as head of the Church of England, could not permit her to marry a divorced man. Under the terms of the Royal Marriages Act the Princess became free of the Queen's veto at the age of 25, but the couple themselves eventually decided that the union could not go ahead for it would have stripped the Princess of her royal rights and prerogatives. As Townsend later said, 'Much as one would like to live on devotion it's just not possible.'

THE QUEEN IN NEW ZEALAND

The Queen and Prince Philip have returned to this country eight times since the December-January 1953-54 and February 1963 tours.

March 1970 saw the first family tour, when Prince Charles and Princess Anne accompanied their parents; four years later the Queen attended and closed the Commonwealth Games in Christchurch; and in February-March 1977 she visited us as part of her Silver Jubilee celebrations.

A short trip followed a Commonwealth Heads of Government conference in Melbourne in October 1981 and another in February-March 1986. Elizabeth was back for her second Commonwealth Games, this time held in Auckland, in February 1990; and returned to the city for the Commonwealth Heads of Government meeting in November 1995.

The Queen's most recent visit took place in February 2002.

OPPOSITE: INFORMAL ATTIRE. IT COULDN'T HAPPEN anywhere other than in New Zealand, or possibly Australia. The Queen and Duke appear unfazed at this meeting with singlet-clad shearers.

Chapter Four

HAPPY FAMILIES

THE MARCH 1970 TOUR LOOKED SET TO BE WRAPPED IN WARM FUZZIES. FOR THE FIRST TIME PRINCE CHARLES AND PRINCESS ANNE WOULD ACCOMPANY THEIR PARENTS TO NEW ZEALAND. FOR THE FIRST TIME WE WOULD SEE THE ROYALS TOGETHER AS A FAMILY.

The younger Princes Andrew and Edward wouldn't be coming, of course. At ages nine and five (Prince Edward would turn six while his parents were away) they would be too much of a handful. Andrew in particular was a boisterous lad. Who knew what sort of mischief he would get up to?

So while New Zealanders looked forward to welcoming the Queen and Duke of Edinburgh for the third time, interest centred mainly on the 21-year-old heir to the throne and his sister, aged 19.

What would they be like? Would Prince Charles be buttoned-up and bashful? Would Princess Anne be as serious and unsmiling as she was sometimes portrayed?

The previous year viewers of the BBC documentary 'The Royal Family' had had a chance to get a close-up look at royalty relaxing at home. In a move that predictably caused some concern, for crusty courtiers feared yet again for the mystique of the monarchy, Elizabeth and Philip opened up their private lives to the television cameras.

People watched in fascination as the family laughed and joked and Philip threw a banger or two on the barbie. Why, they were really quite an ordinary lot – well, in a sort of a way.

'Ordinary' is a word that – surprisingly, perhaps – is not entirely unfamiliar to royals. King George VI and Queen Elizabeth aimed at giving their princesses as ordinary an upbringing as possible. The Queen and Philip attempted to do likewise. Neither succeeded. How could they in a tradition-bound world so vastly different from that of even the most privileged of other British families?

BELOW: BASHFUL? NOT A BIT OF IT. CHARLES MIGHT have looked slightly apprehensive at the start of the tour but he soon thawed out. The *Weekly* reported that 'he always had a smile on his face and a twinkle in his eye' and was a real chip off the old block: 'He even walks just like his dad with his hands clasped behind his back.'

ABOVE: TOGETHERNESS. THE QUEEN, DUKE OF EDINBURGH, Prince Charles and Princess Anne watch intently as children parade their dogs at Southland Agricultural and Pastoral showgrounds in Invercargill during the 1970 'family tour'. A border collie and old English sheepdog featured in the line-up – but, no, there wasn't a corgi in sight.

LEFT: SERIOUS AND UNSMILING? NINETEEN-YEAR-OLD Anne arrived in New Zealand with a reputation for moodiness. And, yes, she did seem a bit glum at first. But we charitably suggested that this was probably due to shyness 'and a feeling of being overwhelmed by masses of people and cameras'.

Thank goodness Prince Charles no longer had to bow to Elizabeth every time he clapped eyes on her (she put a stop to that hitherto essential act of fealty) but unnatural restrictions blighted his early life.

Who could forget the telling 1954 news picture of a small boy welcoming his mother home from abroad with a grave grown-up handshake? The formality of the scene beggared belief. Surely, people thought, any other parent would have at least given her son a kiss!

But Elizabeth wasn't just any mother. At the time she was new to a job she hadn't expected to take on so soon and having to learn the ropes in a hurry. Her early advisors were a hidebound bunch.

There were certain things royals never did in public. To have indulged one's personal feelings, as Princess Diana later did with her children, would have shocked palace sensitivities to the core.

Prince Charles grew into a shy, sensitive child sadly lacking in confidence. This posed problems during his schooldays. While faring well enough with his governess Mispy in the security of the schoolroom at Buckingham Palace (although he was reportedly a slow learner and hopeless at arithmetic), his natural reticence and deep self-consciousness about his royal status made it difficult for him to fit in and relate to classmates at his first two primary schools, Hill House and Cheam. Things got even worse once he arrived at Gordonstoun.

RIGHT: THROWING A BANGER ON the barbie. In 1969 a breakthrough BBC documentary gave television viewers – 23 million of them in Britain alone – a chance to see the royal family relaxing at home. Never before had the royals revealed their off-duty personalities – shirtsleeves rolled up, laughing and joking among themselves.

LEFT: STAYING HOME. A CHARMING 1966 PORTRAIT of Princes Andrew (rear) and Edward. Edward turned six during the two months of the Queen and Prince Philip's 1970 trip Down Under but, as the *Weekly* reported, 'a birthday celebration when their parents are half a world away is not unusual for the royal children, because no reigning monarch has ever undertaken so many overseas tours, and schedules take no note of a small boy's birthday and a mother's desire to be present'.

ABOVE: OFF-DUTY. CHARLES AND ANNE relax at Moose Lodge. Anne displays her famous maxi watch, bought two years earlier at a rustic boutique in Benenden village. She told royal biographer Helen Cathcart, 'I intended it for a few week's fun – but it's still keeping time.'

LEFT: WHAT WAS THAT YOU SAID? A private moment for Elizabeth and Philip at Turangawaewae marae. In what could well have been a royal fashion first, the Queen and Anne – seen just behind her – wear identically styled mother-daughter hats.

This spartan Scottish institution had not been the anxious Queen's choice for her son. She had suggested Eton. But Prince Philip, whom some writers have accused of using bullying tactics, had opted for the school he himself had attended. Philip felt confident that Gordontoun's strict regime of cold showers and brisk outdoor activities in all weathers would make a man of the diffident, home-loving Charles. Charles loathed the place.

In contrast to her brother, Princess Anne is said to have largely enjoyed her schooling. But Anne was an altogether different child. Forceful, outgoing – and often demanding and difficult as well – she mirrored many of her father's characteristics. Unlike the vaguely directionless Charles she also had an all-absorbing hobby, one at which she excelled. Early on she had discovered a passion for horses and at Benenden, which she attended from the age of 13, she was able to take riding lessons and hone the skills that would eventually see her become one of Britain's leading horsewomen.

While his sister galloped away her adolescent frustrations, Charles learned to laugh at his. He later quipped that he'd 'probably have been committed to an institution long ago were it not for the ability to see the funny side of life'.

The royal family gave a glimpse of his particular brand of self-effacing humour when the Prince cheerfully referred to himself on camera as 'a twit'. It also revealed the whole family in modern times as distinctly different from the largely prim-and-proper bunch of popular imagination.

LEFT: SENSITIVE.
Prince Charles, seen here holding little brother Andrew, was shy as a child, sadly lacking in confidence and abnormally eager to please. His obedience in his first classroom at Hill House delighted teachers but worried his parents, who would have liked him to display a bit more get-up-and-go. It was with the idea of fostering independence in the home-loving Prince that they sent him to boarding school, first at Cheam then at Gordonstoun. Charles hated both.

LEFT: FANS. THE QUEEN had plenty of small admirers during the 1970 visit. The scrubbed and smiling faces of the boys in the foreground may well have reminded her of her own two youngsters at home. She missed the little Princes sorely but took comfort from knowing that they'd be getting lots of attention from their loving and often indulgent grandmother, the Queen Mother.

ABOVE: HORSE-MAD. NINE-YEAR-OLD ANNE WITH THE Queen, her pony Greensleeves and corgis Sugar and Whisky at Frogmore in the grounds of Windsor Castle on her birthday in 1959. Unlike her brother, Anne was never short of fighting spirit. As a small child she discovered a passion for horses and went on to become an accomplished and intensely competitive horsewoman. Fearless, too. By the end of 1970 she had sustained a broken finger, a broken nose, two dislocated shoulders and a sprained ankle while competing on the eventing circuit.

ABOVE: HUMOUR. BY HIS OWN ADMISSION, THE HEIR to the throne can afford also to be 'a bit of a twit' from time to time. Charles – seen giving Edward a go-cart ride while the Queen times his performance – once quipped that he would probably have been committed to an institution long ago were it not for his ability to see the funny side of life.

In the lead-up to the 18-day 1970 tour the *Weekly* provided further evidence of just what high-spirited jokers the Windsors could be.

Philip had long been noted for his off-the-cuff witticisms and earthy sometimes foot-in-the-mouth humour. 'Excuse the pong from this end of the room,' he told members of the London Zoological Society, 'your gorilla has just widdled all over me'.

But the Queen a mimic? Apparently, she had a gift for accents and could deliver a credible Ena Sharples 'Eh by gum' or Cockney 'Ow, me poor ole back' as well as send her family into gales of laughter with her broad Scots or Irish brogue.

And it seemed that everyone had a bent for practical jokes. At Cambridge University where he continued his studies after Gordonstoun, Charles had not only taken part in student pranks – one of them saw a statue of Henry VIII sprout an extra pair of arms – but enjoyed custard pie-throwing antics and

'making a bit of a fool of myself' in a variety of skits.

Prince Philip, sporting Dracula fangs, had once chased his shrieking wife through the royal train, and the Queen Mother only narrowly prevented a determined Princess Anne from riding her horse along the hall at Sandringham House and into the royal drawing room.

While this goonish aspect of Windsor life would hardly be on show during the tour, it seemed possible that, given the chance, the royals might be prepared to unbend just a little.

And they did. Princess Anne, who impressed with her trendy tunic trouser suits and glittering evening gowns, seemed a bit glum at first (we charitably suggested that she could be shy as her mother once was), but eventually relaxed; 'the Queen's smiles often stretched into grins' and Prince Philip and Prince Charles 'wisecracked right, left and centre'.

LEFT: MUSIC. AT THE SUPER-POP CONCERT AT WESTERN Springs stadium in Auckland, Anne chats to broadcaster and *Weekly* columnist Cherry Raymond while singer Bunny Walters awaits his turn to meet the Princess.

ABOVE: SPORTY TRIO. AT ST KILDA BEACH, lifesavers get the royal once-over.

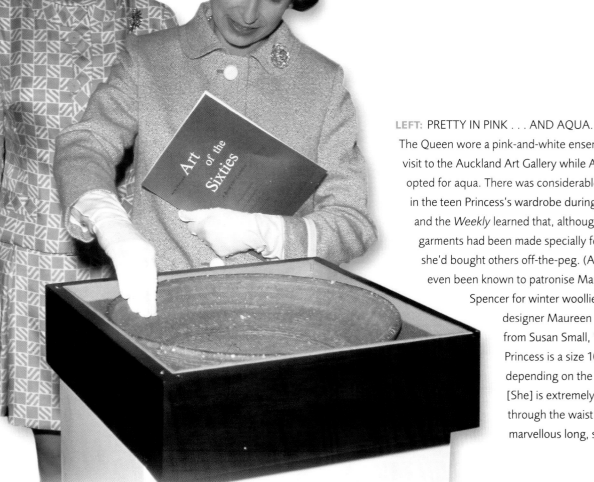

ABOVE LEFT: GLAMOUR. THE QUEEN TALKS TO concertmaster Alex Lindsay after a performance by the NZBC Symphony Orchestra at the Dunedin Town Hall. In the background is a poised Kiri Te Kanawa.

ABOVE RIGHT: SO THAT'S HOW IT'S DONE. THE ROYAL foursome find out how to pan for gold. The Mayor of Queenstown, Warren Cooper, stands at Elizabeth's shoulder.

LEFT: PRETTY IN PINK . . . AND AQUA. The Queen wore a pink-and-white ensemble for a visit to the Auckland Art Gallery while Anne opted for aqua. There was considerable interest in the teen Princess's wardrobe during the tour and the *Weekly* learned that, although some garments had been made specially for her, she'd bought others off-the-peg. (Anne had even been known to patronise Marks & Spencer for winter woollies.) Said designer Maureen Baker from Susan Small, 'The Princess is a size 10 to 12 depending on the style. [She] is extremely slim through the waist with marvellous long, slim legs.'

This was the tour that introduced walkabouts and all four grasped the unprecedented opportunity to chat informally with a wide range of people. It takes poise and confidence to be able to bowl up to strangers and initiate a conversation. But both younger royals appeared to do so with ease.

'Whose twins are those?' Charles asked two nuns standing behind a pram holding the babies. 'They can't be yours.'

When Anne stopped to talk to a four-year-old with a spinal complaint the girl's mother was so enchanted she said impulsively, 'You do look lovely!'

Charles stiff and awkward? Never. Princess Anne bored and gruff? Not that we could see. The royal foursome had turned out to be real charmers and the *Weekly* hailed 'the walkie-talkie people-to-people happening' as the most fun-filled visit yet.

ABOVE: ROYAL DUO. AT THE Investiture held at Wellington Town Hall the Maori Queen Ariki Nui Te Ata-i-Rangikaahu is made a Dame of the British Empire. People sometimes wonder how the Queen copes with what for her would be difficult-to-pronounce names. In Dame Te Ata's case, she studied the correct pronunciation on tape beforehand.

ABOVE: WELL DONE, YOUR MAJESTY! APPLAUSE FROM an onlooker as Elizabeth II leaves Parliament Buildings with Prime Minister Keith Holyoake. Our tour reporter Dorothy Moses also put her hands together for the 'fairytale Queen' whose gorgeous slipper-satin gown with bell-shaped skirt featured a diamond-lattice design embroidered with crystals, pearls and diamonds: she 'wore the Russian Fringe Tiara, which was given to Queen Alexandra on her silver wedding in 1888'.

OPPOSITE: DELIGHT. OUR ROYAL VISITOR DOING WHAT she does so well – smiling. 'It takes years of learning to keep smiling all the time you're on public display,' we said. 'The Queen has learned it well and managed to amaze everyone with her friendly approach. One can imagine the Queen Mother congratulating her when she gets home saying, "You did it this time".'

THE 'LOST' YEARS

Separation from the children had long been part of royal life.

Prince Charles, born in November 1948, was only six months old when the Duke of Edinburgh took up a naval posting in Malta. Princess Elizabeth, as she was then, stayed in London until the little Prince's first birthday before leaving him to join her husband.

Three months after Princess Anne was born in August 1950, Elizabeth again flew out to Malta, not returning to the children until the following March. After only one month at home she left to visit Italy. Later, in 1951, came a tour of North America, followed by the 1952 journey to Kenya which was cut short by the death of King George VI.

At the end of the coronation year the Queen and Prince Philip embarked on a six-month tour of the Commonwealth.

The strain of being separated from Charles and Anne for so long later prompted the Queen to cut back on her overseas duties so that when Prince Andrew arrived in 1960 and Prince Edward in 1964 she and Philip were able to spend more time with the youngsters. Andrew and Edward also benefited from the fact that by this time the Queen felt more confident and relaxed in both her maternal and monarchical roles.

ABOVE: SECOND FAMILY. WHILE THE QUEEN and Prince Philip left their two younger children at home for two months during the 1970 Australia-New Zealand visit, Andrew and Edward did not have to suffer as many parental absences as their older siblings. Andrew, in particular, developed into a fun-loving, often naughty, little boy who aimed his pedal car at the royal corgi pack, put whoopee cushions on his parents' chairs and once tied together the boots of the guardsman outside the palace.

NEW ZEALAND
Woman's Weekly
JULY 27 1981 60c

ROYAL
WEDDING
COUNTDOWN

Chapter Five

HERE COMES
THE BRIDE

QUEEN VICTORIA WOULD NOT HAVE BEEN AMUSED. A PRINCESS MARRYING A COMMONER? A MAN WITH NO TITLE – NOT EVEN A SIR? AND A SOLDIER, TOO! BRING ME MY SMELLING SALTS . . .

But the world had changed drastically in the 100 years since matchmaking Victoria married off her brood. European thrones had fallen. Eligible royals had become increasingly thin on the ground. And in 1973 few, if any, young people would have settled for an arranged marriage, least of all a Princess as wilful and determined as Anne.

Love – that was the only thing that mattered. And it was love that would propel her down the aisle at Westminster Abbey on 14 November to say 'I do' to Captain Mark Phillips.

What the Queen initially thought of the match is not known, although Philip apparently considered Mark a bore. Certainly, by now she was becoming accustomed to seeing family members follow their hearts into commoner territory. Thirteen years earlier Princess Margaret had married society photographer Antony Armstrong-Jones and in 1963 cousin Alexandra had chosen a city businessman as her life partner.

Even so, there were commoners and commoners. And no one who saw the television coverage of Margaret's wedding could have failed to miss the Queen's expression. Elizabeth looked positively glum. It is not hard to imagine why. She must have felt torn. Margaret had lost the only man who, up till now, she had truly loved. This might be her sister's last chance at happiness. How could she possibly have opposed the union? And yet Tony, an arty-crafty bohemian with a decidedly racy past, seemed unsuitable on just about every count. Doubtless she feared for Margaret's long-term happiness.

LEFT: WEDDING BELLE. GORGEOUS BRIDE, A dream of a dress. Princess Margaret poses for an official photograph after her wedding to society photographer Antony Armstrong-Jones in Westminster Abbey on 6 May 1960. The Queen's glum expression throughout the service probably reflected her concern over Margaret's choice of a husband whose free-and-easy bohemian background might spell problems in coping with the restrictions of royal life.

RIGHT: TREND. MARK ANTHONY PETER, do you take this woman Anne Elizabeth Alice Louise to be your lawful wedded wife? When Princess Anne said 'I do' on 14 November 1973 in Westminster Abbey, she continued the trend into commoner territory begun by Princess Margaret. The happy couple walk down the aisle followed by their attendants Lady Sarah Armstrong-Jones and Prince Edward.

THE NEW ZEALAND
Woman's Weekly

DECEMBER 3, 1973

ANNE ➡
& MARK
SOUVENIR
WEDDING
PICTURE

HOW TO GET
YOUR 15 x 20 inch
ENLARGEMENT
OF THIS COVER
PICTURE ON
QUALITY PAPER
SUITABLE
FOR FRAMING

SPECIAL
CHRISTMAS
COOKING
WONDERFUL
RECIPES
FROM OUR
TEST KITCHEN

15c

ABOVE AND BELOW: HANDSOME PAIR. GLITZ AND glamour didn't much interest down-to-earth Princess Anne. Nevertheless, in her dramatic high-necked white silk gown with its wide medieval-styled sleeves she could have stepped straight from the pages of a bridal fashion magazine. Her groom, Captain Mark Phillips, also cut quite a dash in the scarlet and gold tunic of his regiment with its blue velvet collars and cuffs. Because of her desire to live an ordinary life, Anne had wanted a quiet wedding. She didn't get her wish. The nuptials, carried out with appropriate pomp and ceremony, received wide television coverage and sightseers camping out the evening before caused traffic jams along the processional route.

Fortunately, the prospects for her only daughter were much better. Anne and Mark, a £50-a-week captain in the Queen's Dragoon Guards, shared a vital interest – horses. Twenty-five-year-old Mark had been a reserve member of Britain's 1968 Olympic equestrian team. Unlike Tony, he came from a solid country gentry background with no wild goings-on in bachelor pads to worry about. He was robust, good-looking and the often difficult-to-please Anne obviously thought the world of him.

So the Queen smiled happily as she watched the Princess, exquisitely gowned in white silk and pearls, exchange vows in Westminster Abbey with her handsome soldier.

And was that a tear in the royal eye? The *Weekly* thought so. We reported: 'The wedding of Princess Anne and Captain Mark Phillips showed clearly a young couple radiating happiness, a father-of-the-bride who glowed with pride as he walked his daughter up the aisle and a mother-of-the-bride whose eyes grew misty as she saw her only daughter emerge from the vestry a married woman.'

ABOVE: MISTY-EYED? THE QUEEN shows delight, with perhaps a hint of happy tears, as her only daughter emerges from the vestry a married woman. The *Weekly* sought permission to photograph proceedings direct from one of the new colour television screens (there were only 8000 licensed sets in New Zealand at the time) in order to bring pictures to readers as quickly as possible.

ABOVE AND LEFT: PASSION. THEY MIGHT have come from different social strata, but Mark Phillips and Princess Anne had something important in common – a passion for horses. From the Queen's point of view, this probably boded well for their future happiness. The newlyweds are seen here on honeymoon, and in New Zealand during their February 1974 visit.

ABOVE AND LEFT: SO HAPPY. THE Queen's cousin Princess Alexandra and her businessman husband the Hon Angus Ogilvy showed just how happy the marriage between a royal and a commoner could be. The couple tied the knot in 1963 and eight years later visited New Zealand where their informality and easy-going charm won them many friends.

Eight years later the Queen was smiling again. And with even greater cause. In the first place, she must have been vastly relieved that 32-year-old Charles, who for years had drifted from one girlfriend to another without getting anywhere near the altar, had finally settled on a bride. Second, she cannot have failed to applaud his choice. Everybody approved! It seemed that the whole world had gone crazy over the sweet and lovely 19-year-old Lady Diana Spencer.

On 29 July 1981 the world went crazier still as the shy former kindergarten assistant, gowned in a confection of ivory silk and old lace hand embroidered with tiny mother-of-pearl sequins and pearls, nervously promised to take Charles Philip Arthur George (unfortunately she got it round the wrong way and said Philip Charles) to be her wedded husband.

The *Weekly* pulled out all the adjectival stops – the bride, 'pale, pure, and downright pretty . . . a slim ivory vision'; the groom, 'dashing in royal navy blue'; the gown, 'a froth of frills, flounces . . . a sheer delight'; and the wedding itself, 'a dream – the sort from which fairy tales are made'.

Never before had there been a royal wedding that so captured public imagination – television had brought every enchanting moment, including the famous kiss on the Buckingham Palace balcony, to an estimated 750 million people – and it seemed unlikely that such spell-binding magnificence could ever be repeated.

RIGHT: THE WEDDING OF THE CENTURY. THANKS TO television, the eyes of the world were on Prince Charles and Lady Diana Spencer as they exchanged vows in St Paul's Cathedral on the morning of 29 July 1981. The *Weekly* described 'Shy Di' as young, glowing and looking like a dream in her 'wildly feminine' silk and lace gown and detachable train, the longest in royal history, which trailed fully 7.5 metres behind her.

ROYAL WEDDING COUNTDOWN

LEFT: WELL-MATCHED. HE COULDN'T have chosen better! That's what the world thought when it learned in 1981 that Prince Charles was to marry shy kindergarten assistant Lady Diana Spencer. Not only was Lady Di drop-dead gorgeous, she had the right aristocratic credentials: the Spencer family had long moved in royal circles. Her father, the eighth Earl Spencer had been equerry to George VI while her grandmother Ruth, Lady Fermoy, was both lady-in-waiting to the Queen Mother and one of her closest friends.

ABOVE: FAMOUS PHOTO. THIS SOUVENIR PLAQUE FEATURES the official engagement picture of Charles and his bride-to-be. Lady Diana wears a somewhat frumpish royal blue suit – her final off-the-peg purchase before the fashion gurus took her in hand.

ABOVE: SERIOUS QUEEN. PRINCESS ANNE AND HUSBAND
Mark Phillips exchange warm glances during Charles and Diana's
wedding ceremony but the rest of the family (including Lord
Linley, top right) appear distinctly solemn. After the signing of the
register, however, the Queen broke into a broad smile and the
Queen Mother wept unashamedly. It seemed that wedding
nerves hadn't been confined to Diana (who had muffed her
responses and muddled Charles' name). Elizabeth had been
concerned for the health of Diana's father, Earl Spencer, who had
not fully recovered from a massive brain haemorrhage and at
times had looked near to collapse.

RIGHT: UNDERCURRENTS. THE PRINCE AND PRINCESS OF
Wales leave St Paul's, amid wild cheering, for the return
journey to Buckingham Palace. The wedding saw an
enormous gathering of royals and other VIPs. However,
animosity between Diana and her bossy stepmother Raine,
Countess Spencer, was reflected in the seating arrangements
which put the Countess among the general congregation.
Raine's mother, romantic novelist Barbara Cartland, received
an even greater snub. She failed to get an invitation.

But in March 1986 excitement began mounting once more. The Queen's second son, Prince Andrew, had popped the question. In July it would be the turn of red-haired 26-year-old Sarah Ferguson, the daughter of Prince Charles' polo manager, to take centre stage.

Unlike Princess Diana, Sarah did not have to meet the virginal qualification essential for the bride of the heir to the throne. She'd lived a bit. She was bold, bouncy and exuded confidence.

The Queen and Prince Philip liked her. They believed the unpretentious, down-to-earth Fergie would be just the partner to tame a cocksure and somewhat immature son given to boisterous pranks and dalliances with unsuitable women such as soft-porn actress Koo Stark.

The Queen Mother added her approval. She thought Sarah 'a delightful girl'.

So the 'delightful girl' – every inch a beautiful bride in her gown of rich, ivory silk duchesse satin with pearl trim – exchanged vows with her sailor Prince in Westminster Abbey and, just as they had five years earlier for the Prince and Princess of Wales, Londoners gave the couple a rapturous reception.

The wedding might not have achieved quite the magic of Charles and Diana's nuptials but it scored full marks for sheer, unalloyed happiness. The *Weekly* reported: 'There was pomp and ceremony aplenty but little or no sign of stiffness, starchiness or nerves. In fact, the marriage of the Duke and Duchess of York [as they now were] was perhaps one of the most joyful royal occasions ever.'

ABOVE: CONTROVERSY. ALTHOUGH THE *WEEKLY* WAXED LYRICAL OVER THE Princess of Wales' cream-puff wedding gown, which we described as totally daring, wildly feminine and a sheer delight, not everyone agreed. It was noticeable that the vast skirt crushed easily and some fashion commentators slammed the Elizabeth and David Emanuel creation as overblown and over-the-top. The bodice had evidently been taken in several times during the preceding weeks to cope with weight loss brought on by the bride's pre-wedding nerves. And was that a smile of relief as the new Princess, together with Charles, the Queen and Earl Spencer made a farewell appearance on the Buckingham Palace balcony?

LEFT: BONANZA. WE CELEBRATED THE ROYAL LOVE MATCH WITH A 10-page wedding special. Three hundred thousand copies of the magazine were printed and the issue was a virtual sell-out.

LEFT: FERGIE'S TURN. COULD THE wedding of Prince Andrew and Sarah Ferguson possibly repeat the special magic of Charles and Diana's extravaganza? Red-haired Fergie (Andrew called the colour Titian) lacked Diana's delicate loveliness, but she was lively, outgoing, full of fun and, given the expertise of fashion designer Lindka Cierach, was bound to be a beautiful bride.

POSTAL TRIBUTES

LEFT: WEDDING OF THE century. The Post Office marked the happy event with stamps featuring the newlyweds and St Paul's Cathedral.

ABOVE: GOOD SPORTS. THE SMILING FACES OF ANDREW AND SARAH joined five sets of powerful legs on stamps depicting Commonwealth Games themes on this envelope mailed to New Zealand in July 1986.

ABOVE: HAPPINESS ALL THE WAY. That's how the *Weekly* summarised Andrew and Sarah's nuptials on 23 July 1986. Britain's second royal bride of the 1980s showed not the slightest sign of shyness or nerves. She neither blushed nor trembled. This was her day and together with her groom she obviously enjoyed every minute! Needless to say, Lindka Cierach did her client proud. Sarah's classically-styled gown of ivory silk duchesse satin with pearl trim featured beadwork depicting thistles and honeybees, the bee and thistle being the principal images on her personal coat of arms. At 5.3 metres, her train was considerably shorter than Diana's record-breaker.

Three down and one to go. The years marched on. The Queen's youngest son hit his 30s with no sign of settling down. Edward had a girlfriend, a PR executive who had once promoted Mr Blobby. He had met Sophie Rhys-Jones in 1993, but the couple seemed curiously laid back. None of Shy Di's adoring sideways glances or Andrew and Sarah's exuberant horseplay in this relationship! It was not until 1999 that Edward got a move on and preparations for the final royal wedding of the 20th century began.

This, however, was to be a very different affair, for it was held not in St Paul's Cathedral or Westminster Abbey but in St George's Chapel, Windsor Castle, with a 550-strong guest list geared more toward friends – who included television and showbiz folk – than foreign dignitaries. In another departure, the ceremony itself began in the late afternoon, thus relieving guests of the necessity to wear hats (although the Queen Mother arrived in her usual headgear and the Queen compromised with a halo of feathers).

As if to underline the comparatively low-key atmosphere of the occasion, a relaxed and confident Edward winked at his bride-to-be – serene and lovely in a long, fitted coatdress trimmed with pearls and crystal beading – as she arrived at the altar. And later the couple giggled when her wedding ring had to be forced on to a finger swollen in the summer heat.

The *Weekly* commented: 'Anybody who had ever wondered if Prince Edward was reluctant to marry Sophie Rhys-Jones only had to look at his face to see that he was telling the truth the night before his wedding when he said, "We happen to love each other which is the most important thing of all."'

ABOVE: LOVEBIRDS. THE NEWLY CONFERRED EARL OF Wessex and his Countess acknowledge the cheers of well-wishers. While embodying much of the pomp and pageantry of a traditional royal wedding, the couple's big day on 19 June 1999 was noted for its informal touches. Sophie wore a comparatively simple ivory silk and organza coatdress trimmed with rows of pearls and crystal beads.

ABOVE: TOGETHERNESS. THE HAPPY COUPLE HOLD HANDS as they pose for photographers. Sophie's pearl necklace and matching earrings were a wedding present from Prince Edward. Her tiara came from the Queen's private collection.

LEFT: FAMILY PHOTO. THE wedding party on the chapel steps. The bride's mother Mary, in an orange ensemble, is behind the two little bridesmaids whose velvet tunics match those of the pages. Prince Andrew can be seen to the left of Edward, while Prince William stands above Prince Charles, who is partly obscured by Sophie. The Queen, who had been relaxed and happy throughout the service, appears somewhat subdued. Possibly she was worried about the stiff breeze which ruffled hairdos and threatened to lift skirts.

PRINCES, DUKES AND EARLS

ABOVE: NO ROYAL TITLE. PRINCESS ALEXANDRA and her husband, the Hon Angus Ogilvy, in New Zealand in 1971. The fiercely independent Ogilvy had been offered an earldom but refused it on the grounds that he didn't see why marriage to a Princess should qualify him for a peerage.

A royal wedding often signals a change of status in more ways than one. On his marriage to Princess Elizabeth, Philip Mountbatten became the Duke of Edinburgh. (It is often not realised that the Queen is also the Duchess of Edinburgh.)

Antony Armstrong-Jones did not see why marriage to Princess Margaret should qualify him for ennoblement, but he finally bowed to pressure and from 1961 was known as the Earl of Snowdon. Mark Phillips, on the other hand, stuck to his guns and, with Princess Anne's approval, declined the Queen's offer of a title.

In 1981 Lady Diana Spencer stepped into St Paul's Cathedral and emerged as the Princess of Wales, and in 1986 Sarah Ferguson became the Duchess of York, Prince Andrew having been made the Duke of York the day before their wedding.

The Queen had been expected to honour Edward with a dukedom on his marriage to Sophie Rhys-Jones. Instead she chose to make him the Earl of Wessex and Sophie became his Countess.

Chapter Six

UNHAPPY FAMILIES

'WE HAPPEN TO LOVE EACH OTHER WHICH IS THE MOST IMPORTANT THING OF ALL.' YES, BUT LOVE CAN SOMETIMES FAIL. AND BY THE TIME PRINCE EDWARD UTTERED THESE WORDS IT HAD COME TO GRIEF SPECTACULARLY IN THE HOUSE OF WINDSOR.

Of her immediate family, only the Queen had managed to keep her marriage together. She had to, of course. For her, marriage really did mean 'until death us do part'. There could be no wriggling out when the going got tough.

And the going probably did get tough at times. Elizabeth hadn't married the easiest person in the world. Philip had found difficulty adjusting to his second-fiddle role. He was his own man. He wanted to do his own thing (he'd had to give up the naval career he loved) and handshaking and hobnobbing with stuffy officials were not exactly part of it. Frustration could make him rude and irascible. Elizabeth, for her part, had to find a balance between being a call-the-shots monarch and a wife who had promised to 'love, honour and obey'. But somehow the couple had overcome their difficulties and built a partnership that grew stronger with the years.

If Elizabeth and Philip could do it, why couldn't the others?

RIGHT: 'THE HAPPIEST TOUR'. THE *WEEKLY* SALUTES THE ROYAL COUPLE. Although the Queen's marriage has largely escaped the attention of scandalmongers, there have been suggestions from time to time – although never any proof – that the Duke's attentions might have strayed elsewhere.

LEFT: HAPPY, BUT . . . EVEN A HAPPY MARRIAGE CAN experience problems. The Duke of Edinburgh, a workaholic who had to give up the naval career he loved when Elizabeth became Queen, had difficulty adjusting to his second-fiddle role. Wisely, the Queen gave him his head to pursue his own interests – largely connected with science and technology – and appeared not to object when he let off steam with boisterous buddies from his navy days. The royal couple are seen with daughter Princess Anne in New Zealand in 1970.

ABOVE: ENQUIRING MIND. THE DUKE OF EDINBURGH deep in conversation. He enjoys meeting people from manufacturing and industry and is equally at home with workers and bosses.

ABOVE: POLO ENTHUSIAST. PHILIP'S EARLIER PASSION for polo (nowadays he enjoys the more sedate carriage-driving) has been inherited by son Charles. Diana sometimes described herself as a polo widow.

In Princess Margaret's case the answer is not hard to find. The Queen's sister was pigheaded and spoiled, accustomed to being waited on hand and foot and getting her own way. Her equally stubborn husband insisted on retaining his independence and refused to be ordered about or forced into a royal mould. Once passion died (in their courting days it was said the couple couldn't keep their hands off each other) little else remained. Margaret turned to rakish high-society charmer Robin Douglas-Home for comfort, then struck up an improbable liaison with shaggy-haired part-time gardener Roddy Llewellyn.

When news of the Roddy affair became public – as it did in 1976, the year Margaret and Tony finally separated – the public chortled. Plump middle-aged Margaret cavorting about with a hippie 17 years her junior? Ridiculous! How the Queen must have shuddered.

But Margaret's marriage break-up was just the beginning. Ten years later Elizabeth faced another family crisis, this one even closer to home. Princess Anne and Mark Phillips had been so in love on their wedding day. He had looked dishy in his scarlet uniform and she had gazed adoringly into his eyes. But love had cooled in a climate of increasing disdain on bossy, quick-witted Anne's part for a husband whose slower

reactions had earned him the somewhat unkind nickname of Fog (thick and wet). By the mid-80s the Phillips' marriage had become a sham and Anne approached the Queen for permission to end it. While reportedly sad but not surprised at the request, Elizabeth hesitated. Princess Margaret's divorce in 1978 had been the first in the British royal family since Henry VIII had gone on a wife-dispatching spree in the 16th century. She did not relish the thought of another dissolution so soon.

Two events may have finally forced her hand. It seemed that Mark had gone seriously astray; in 1989 came the shock claim that he had fathered a love child in New Zealand. And the downmarket tabloid the *Sun* somehow got hold of intimate letters written to Anne by the Queen's equerry, Commander Timothy Laurence. While trumpeting its find, the paper – not usually noted for reticence – baulked at publishing so much as a single excerpt, thus giving the impression that the contents must have been really hot stuff.

With Mark in the royal black books and Anne carrying a torch for someone else, the marriage which romantic novelist Barbara Cartland had described as a 'historical experiment' had sustained its final blow. A legal separation followed and the couple later divorced.

RIGHT: ILL-MATCHED. A SEEMINGLY happy Princess Margaret, Lord Snowdon and their six-year-old son Viscount Linley leave St George's Chapel, Windsor Castle, after the 1967 Christmas morning service. Independent-minded Tony hated his Snowdon title (he'd been forced into accepting it) and resisted attempts to make him conform to royal rules. He also resented having to live at Kensington Palace, which he regarded as charity from the Queen. Princess Margaret, by contrast, thoroughly enjoyed her royal status and all that went with it. Accustomed to being praised and getting her own way, she had trouble coping with the give and take of marriage. The couple had two children, the younger of whom, Lady Sarah Armstrong-Jones, was born in 1964.

LEFT: NEWLYWEDS. PRINCESS Anne and Captain Mark Phillips had been married less than three months when they visited New Zealand, where they attended the 1974 Commonwealth Games in Christchurch. By the mid-80s, however, their smiles had faded and when the couple went to Los Angeles for the Olympics in 1984 they stayed at different hotels some 50 km apart.

RIGHT: THE OTHER MAN. WITH HER MARRIAGE to Mark little more than a sham, Anne found an outlet for her affections in the Queen's equerry, Commander Timothy Laurence. The Princess's love for Laurence, together with Mark's New Zealand liaison, finally put an end to the couple's union. Anne and Mark separated in 1989 and two years later Anne married her lover. Anne, Tim and Zara Phillips are seen outside St George's Chapel, Windsor Castle, in 1993.

LEFT: LOVER. PRINCESS MARGARET'S AFFAIR WITH PART-TIME garden designer Roddy Llewellyn – an emotionally fragile man young enough to be her son – scandalised other members of the royal family. Roddy spent holidays with the middle-aged Princess at her second home on Mustique in the Caribbean and she in her turn visited him at his hippie commune, a decidedly free-and-easy establishment where guests sometimes ran around in the nude. The relationship – tolerated for a time by Tony, who also enjoyed extramarital amours – eventually brought the curtain down on the Snowdon marriage. Princess Margaret and Lord Snowdon separated in 1976.

Meanwhile, the Duke and Duchess of York had begun to cause headaches in royal circles. The hope that flame-haired Fergie might help curb her husband's irresponsible tendencies had proved wide of the mark. She simply egged Andrew on. Together the ebullient couple cheerfully thumbed their noses at royal protocols and proceeded to follow a life of silliness and excess. Dignity? What was that? Sarah did not appear to know the meaning of the word. Poking male friends in the buttocks with an umbrella at Ascot was not the sort of behaviour expected from a 27-year-old Princess.

The press, which initially hailed Fergie as bringing a breath of fresh air to the fusty House of Windsor, turned against her. Commentators ridiculed her fashion sense, generous proportions (one cruelly labelled her the Duchess of Pork), enthusiasm for holidays and spending sprees. Not even Sarah's taste in interior decor escaped critical comment. The Yorks' home, Sunninghill Park – built for them by the Queen at a cost of some £5 million – was slammed for its vulgar ostentation and quickly dubbed South York, after the South Fork residence of the television series *Dallas*. The Duchess of Pork at South York. What an embarrassment for the Queen!

But worse was to come. With naval officer Andrew regularly away from home – Sarah later claimed the couple spent less than 50 days together each year – the restless Duchess sought other outlets for her affections. American Steve Wyatt filled the bill nicely and later her financial advisor John Bryan demonstrated talents far removed from an ability to add up figures.

It was unlikely that Sarah's indiscretions could have remained secret for long. They didn't. By the early 90s the Queen became aware that high jinks in the Yorks' marriage had taken a different and decidedly dangerous turn – as if she didn't already have enough to worry about with Charles and Diana.

BELOW: ABSENCE. IT IS SAID THAT ABSENCE MAKES THE heart grow fonder. In the Duchess of York's case it grew fonder of others. With Andrew away on naval duty, and feeling like a fish out of water in the royal system, Sarah turned first to wealthy American Steve Wyatt and then to her financial advisor John Bryan for affection and reassurance.

ABOVE: FLAK. SUNNINGHILL PARK, THE HOME OF THE DUKE and Duchess of York, drew derisive comments for its ostentatious opulence. Fergie found herself in the firing line, as well. Fashion gurus jeered at her generous proportions (she ballooned to size 20 during her pregnancy with Princess Beatrice in 1988) and taste in clothes and hairstyles (she wore a ponytail during an official visit to Canada). Others criticised her choice of friends and reliance on advice from fortune-tellers and astrologers.

BELOW: TENSION. AM I DOING IT CORRECTLY THIS time? The Duchess of York's disregard for royal protocols usually met with her husband's enthusiastic approval. Indeed, she egged him on to similarly unroyal behaviour. Sometimes, however, the ebullient Fergie made a public gaffe that so irritated Andrew he'd tick her off then and there. Not surprisingly, she felt utterly humiliated.

The marital difficulties of the Prince and Princess of Wales have been well documented. To New Zealanders the first hints in the late 1980s that all might not be sweetness and light in the fairytale marriage came as a sad surprise. After all, the couple had seemed so happy together when they toured the country in 1983. Who could forget the charming photograph of Charles and Diana with Prince William in the grounds of Government House in Auckland? It had depicted such a homely scene – Mum and Dad sitting on a rug on the lawn, little Prince playing with a Buzzy Bee toy. Later we learned that Diana had been desperately unhappy at the time; that she'd felt inadequate, insecure and unappreciated; that she suspected her husband of having an affair; and that she was already susceptible to the bulimia that would plague her in years to come. Yet she had never given the slightest indication of her inner turmoil. Even in those early days Diana had successfully mastered the royal rule: no matter how wretched you felt, you never gave so much as a hint in public. You smiled and kept smiling.

LEFT: PRINCESS PERFECT. SHE might have been unsure of her husband's heart, but in 1983 Princess Diana captured the hearts of thousands of others. The *Weekly* wrote: 'Her touch seems to have the effect of a fairy wand . . . her hand becomes red from shaking other people's.'

RIGHT: UPSTAGED. CHARLES AND Diana with Prince Edward, who had been tutoring at Wanganui Collegiate. Accustomed to being the centre of attention, Charles discovered when he came to New Zealand that it was the gorgeous Diana people wanted to see. While appearing to accept the situation with good grace, he reportedly felt miffed.

LEFT: WARNING. NOT EVERYONE SAW CHARLES AND DIANA'S union as a marriage made in heaven. Psychologists Bradford Wilson and George Edington warned of personality clashes. Charles, they said, was less cool, calm and collected than people imagined, and apt to be competitive with women. Diana was subject to mood swings – very up when things were going her way, very down when they weren't.

BELOW: HAPPY. DIANA – SEEN HERE WITH CHARLES AND LITTLE William – looked so happy during her 1983 New Zealand visit. However, appearances can deceive and at the time she harboured serious doubts about her ability to perform her roles as both Princess and wife. The *Weekly* detected her vulnerability. We noted that she seemed 'as fragile, almost, as a single bruised daisy accepted from a child'.

The Queen, of course, was – and is – a past master of the art. Family troubles? Nobody observing Elizabeth as she and the Duke of Edinburgh acknowledged the delight of huge crowds during walkabouts in New Zealand in 1986 would have guessed it. Not even an egg-throwing incident could ruffle her composure. ('What's that?' said a youngster pointing to a smear on the royal coat. 'Oh, it's an egg, dear.') Yet by then the Queen was well aware of the sterile nature of Princess Anne's marriage and obviously had some knowledge of the strife in the Prince and Princess of Wales' household.

By the time she arrived in this country, her usual smiling self, to take part in events marking the sesquicentennial of the Treaty of Waitangi in 1990, she probably suspected that the union of the Duke and Duchess of York might also be sailing into troubled waters.

Normally a Queen does not comment in public on private concerns. But in 1992 Elizabeth was forced to admit that life for the House of Windsor had become decidedly 'horribilis'.

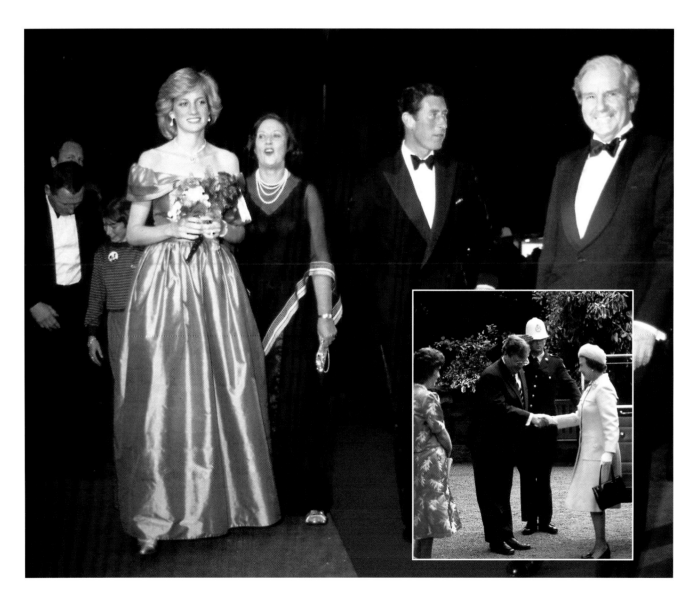

ABOVE: SO SLENDER. NOBODY REALISED IT AT THE TIME BUT BY 1983 Diana was already suffering from the slimming disease bulimia. She and Prince Charles are accompanied here by Alan Highet, Minister of Internal Affairs, and his wife, the artist and author Shona McFarlane.

INSET ABOVE: HER USUAL SMILING SELF. PRIVATE worries? Nobody would have guessed it during the Queen's 1986 visit. Here she is welcomed by Prime Minister David Lange and his wife Naomi.

ABOVE: COMPOSURE. NOT EVEN AN EGG-THROWING incident in Auckland in 1986 could disturb Elizabeth's aplomb. Wellington fans assured her that she need have no fear of a repeat performance in the capital.

ABOVE: FOCUSED. THE QUEEN RESPONDS TO A SPEECH of welcome at celebrations to mark the sesquicentennial of the signing of the Treaty of Waitangi in 1990. By this time Anne and Mark had separated, Charles and Diana's marriage was in deep trouble, and fun and games in the Yorks' household had taken a new and dangerous turn.

ABOVE: FAITH. ELIZABETH HAS A DEEP SPIRITUAL faith and, despite her children's marital disasters, remains a believer in the importance of the family unit.

FAMILY EXAMPLE

If the Queen was troubled by Princess Margaret's divorce – as indeed she was – she must have been devastated over her children's subsequent marital disasters, for she believed that marriage should be a lifelong commitment.

In 1978 Dr Mervyn Stockwood, then Bishop of Southwark and someone she obviously knew well, outlined her views. Writing in London's Evening Standard, *he said: 'The Queen is an out-and-out supporter of the Church in its insistence upon the importance of the family unit. She has an understanding attitude towards the weaknesses of human nature but this does not shake her conviction that the nation runs into troubled water when the family unit disintegrates. She is not just a believer. She practises what she preaches. Anyone who has anything to do with her family circle knows what a precious thing it is to her.'*

Chapter Seven

ANNUS HORRIBILIS

THE QUEEN HAD THE FLU AND A TEMPERATURE OF 101 DEGREES FAHRENHEIT. BUT THAT WASN'T ABOUT TO STOP HER FULFILLING HER APPOINTMENT TO ADDRESS A BANQUET ON THE EVENING OF 24 NOVEMBER 1992 AT THE GUILDHALL IN THE CITY OF LONDON. BESIDES, FLU WAS THE LEAST OF HER WORRIES.

I n a hoarse voice she told her audience that this was 'not a year on which I will look back with undiluted pleasure. In the words of one of my more sympathetic correspondents, it has turned out to be an annus horribilis.'

The first indication that the Queen was about to endure what the *Sun* newspaper rudely dubbed 'one's bum year' came in March with the announcement that the Duke and Duchess of York were to separate. Ostensibly, sassy Sarah had failed to adjust to the restrictions of royal life. She said she'd felt like a caged bird. But the fact that the break-up came shortly after the publication of snapshots depicting Texan oil tycoon Steve Wyatt playing 'Uncle Stevie' to little Princess Beatrice during a secret holiday with the Duchess in the south of France suggested a more immediate cause. Later in August Andrew's wayward wife sent further shock waves through the royal family when raunchy photographs taken during a second French holiday surfaced in the media. The paparazzi shots showed a topless Fergie being kissed and nuzzled from head to foot — with special attention to the toes — by her financial advisor John Bryan while her daughters Beatrice and Eugenie played nearby.

ABOVE: GREAT EXPECTATIONS. AT THE START of 1992 the Queen had every reason to feel upbeat. February 6 marked the 40th anniversary of a highly successful reign, and there would be plenty of celebrations in the coming months. But neither Elizabeth nor anyone else suspected what horrors the fates had in store.

ABOVE: OH DEAR! BEFORE JANUARY WAS out the Duchess of York (seen here with the infant Princess Beatrice) blotted her copybook. A snapshot of Beatrice on the knee of oil tycoon Steve Wyatt, taken during a secret holiday and published in one of the tabloids, suggested that the Duchess's relationship with 'Uncle Stevie' had gone beyond mere friendship.

BELOW: MARRIAGE OVER. THE Duchess of York had had enough, and some commentators pointed the finger at the British tabloids. Not only had 'the bloody vultures' (Philip's expression) hounded Fergie about her appearance, her boisterous jolly hockey-sticks manner, lavish spending, freebie holidays and unsuitable friends, but they'd even tried to poke their noses into her bedroom. In March the Palace announced that the Duke and Duchess of York were to separate.

April saw Princess Anne's 18-year-old marriage end in a four-minute quickie divorce, but it was Andrew Morton's June bombshell, a tell-all biography of the Princess of Wales, that really sent blood pressures soaring at Buckingham Palace. Not only did *Diana: Her True Story* expose the desperate loneliness and sense of worthlessness that fuelled the vulnerable Princess's bulimia and drove her to several suicide attempts, it also did a thorough hatchet job on the Prince of Wales. According to Diana – or rather, the friends who spoke on her behalf to Morton – Charles had turned out to be a cold, uncaring, insensitive and self-absorbed husband who offered no support and who went out of the way to distance himself from the wife he heartily grew to dislike. Needless to say, Prince Charles was livid at what he saw as the ultimate betrayal. And it may be assumed that his mother saw red as well, although Diana later strongly denied any rift with the Queen and Prince Philip.

But the die had been cast. The already considerable speculation about Charles and Diana's private lives (some of it had started in Britain as far back as 1982) rapidly gained momentum. A February photograph of a soulful Princess all alone at the Taj Mahal, the world's greatest monument to love, had painted a poignant portrait of loneliness. Could Morton's informants be correct? Could the marriage really have reached the point of no return? Confirmation was not long in coming – and with it, further embarrassment for the Queen.

In August details of a taped telephone conversation between Diana and friend James Gilbey hit the news-stands. In it the besotted Gilbey called her 'Squidgy' and professed his love while she in her turn confessed her unhappiness and spoke disparagingly about Charles and her royal in-laws. The following month the tabloids engaged in feverish speculation about a possible relationship between the princess and a man mentioned briefly in Morton's book, Major James Hewitt. And in November during a trip to Korea Charles and Diana appeared to be so down-at-the mouth and utterly bored with each other that reporters tagged them 'The Glums'.

LEFT AND CENTRE: SHOCK, HORROR! PUBLICATION IN JUNE OF ANDREW Morton's biography *Diana: Her True Story* raised Palace blood pressure to boiling point. Morton claimed that the Princess felt trapped in a loveless marriage; that loneliness had brought her to the edge of despair; and that she had made a number of suicide attempts. He also revealed that she suffered from bulimia nervosa and felt like an outsider within the royal system.

ABOVE: *DALLAS* AT THE PALACE. Will Diana leave Charles? Can Andrew win Fergie back? Is Anne headed for marriage number two? The *Weekly* had the (possible) answers.

ABOVE: AT THE END OF THEIR TETHER. CHARLES TURNS AWAY; DIANA'S shoulders are slumped and her face is the picture of misery. This photograph of the royal couple in Korea saw them labelled 'the Glums'.

BELOW: LOVER. SEPTEMBER SAW Diana's friend Major James Hewitt issue a libel writ in the High Court after days of feverish speculation about his relationship with the Princess. It later transpired that Hewitt had indeed been Diana's lover. In her famous *Panorama* television interview she declared, 'I adored him.'

ABOVE: NOT OUR DI!
The *Weekly* delivered its verdict on claims that Diana had attempted suicide.

ABOVE: PRISONER. ANDREW Morton revealed that the Princess had paid a high price for her royal status and dreamed of the day she could 'run along a beach without a policeman following me'.

If the Queen's formidable composure had been put to the test by these unfortunate developments it was in for an even greater challenge. For in that same month the *Daily Mirror* published excerpts from a steamy telephone conversation – actually secretly recorded in December 1989 – between Prince Charles and his long-time friend Mrs Camilla Parker Bowles.

The taped exchange provided proof positive (in language and imagery more suited to an airport paperback than the heir to the throne) of Charles's infidelity; proof positive that, as Diana would later say, 'there were three of us in this marriage'.

Of course, royal bad behaviour is hardly new. Not for nothing was the Queen's great-grandfather Edward VII dubbed Edward the Caresser. But 90 years ago there had been no listening devices to record the libidinous King's amorous murmurings to his mistress Mrs Keppel. Similarly Edward's dissolute son, the Duke of Clarence, went about his dubious activities (he was said to have patronised a homosexual brothel) free from the intrusion of telephoto lenses. The public also remained in blissful ignorance of the antics of the brothers of the future George VI – David's dalliances with married women and George, Duke of Kent's flirtation with drugs.

ABOVE: WHAT DOES HE SEE IN HER? THAT WAS THE question people asked after the *Mirror* claimed that Prince Charles had revived his love affair with former flame, 43-year-old Camilla Parker Bowles. Camilla might have been a jolly, horse-loving sort, but in appearance and charm could not hold a candle to the gorgeous Diana. Brigadier Parker Bowles, Director of the Royal Army Veterinary Corps, initially dismissed reports of the liaison as fiction.

ABOVE: ROUÉ. ROYAL BAD BEHAVIOUR IS NOTHING NEW. The Queen's libidinous great-grandfather, Edward VII, embarrassed his long-suffering wife, Queen Alexandra, throughout their marriage with a string of affairs, often with the wives of friends. His most famous paramours included Lillie Langtry, Daisy, Lady Brooke and Alice Keppel.

BELOW: SQUIDGY. IT IS UNLIKELY THAT – EVEN IN THE EARLY DAYS – CHARLES ever had an affectionate pet name for Princess Diana. But her friend James Gilbey certainly did. Published details of a taped telephone conversation in which Gilbey told his 'Squidgy' that he couldn't face the thought of not speaking to her every moment, and Diana maintained that Charles made her life real torture, added to the shocks of 1992 and doubtless the Queen's distress.

ABOVE: ACID RAINE. PRINCESS Diana's cool relationship with her stepmother, Raine, Countess Spencer, had long been an open secret. But until 1992 the extent of the Princess's antipathy toward the woman dubbed Acid Raine had never been revealed. The *Weekly* commented: 'Doubtless [our story] will shock, but it may also remind us that even the saintliest of Princesses can crack under the strain of family tensions.'

ABOVE: FERGIE, HOW COULD YOU? THE DUCHESS OF YORK believed that separation gave her the red light to go her own sweet way and associate with whomever she liked in whatever way she chose.

But in 1992 royals lived in the glare of the unforgiving spotlight. No caring mother could fail to be distressed by the breakdown of her children's marriages. But ordinary mothers do not have to watch the marriages in question being publicly dissected; the difficulties and misdemeanours of the participants detailed – sometimes with lip-smacking relish – in page after page of print. How it must have wounded the Queen to see herself described as the head of the world's most dysfunctional family.

Surely nothing more could go wrong. But 20 November delivered an entirely unexpected blow. Windsor Castle, the Queen's weekend home, caught fire and severely damaged the St George's Hall, Grand Reception Room, Private Chapel, State Dining Room, Crimson Drawing Room and various subsidiary rooms. She was devastated. Press photographs depicted a desolate Elizabeth, head bowed, as she turned away from the unbearable sight of the historic Brunswick Tower engulfed in flames.

LEFT: INFERNO. AS IF FAMILY troubles weren't enough, the Queen's annus horribilis also saw historic Windsor Castle, her weekend home, partially destroyed by fire. Eight hours after the fire first took hold in the Private Chapel at the north-east angle of the upper ward, 12-m flames erupted like a volcano from the Brunswick Tower.

RIGHT: DEVASTATION. Although a rescue effort led by Prince Andrew saved works of art and other priceless treasures in the 900-year-old Windsor Castle, more than 100 rooms, including St George's Hall and the Grand Reception Room, were either damaged or destroyed. Two hundred and fifty fire-fighters took 15 hours and used 6.8 million litres of water to put out the fire.

SECURITY SCARE

It might not have been an annus horribilis but 1982 had its share of shocking events.

On the morning of 9 July the Queen woke suddenly to find a stranger with a bleeding hand standing by her bed. Unemployed labourer Michael Fagan had somehow managed to penetrate Buckingham Palace security and land up in the royal bedroom.

Another woman might have screamed blue murder. Not the Queen. After an alarm bell and two telephone calls failed to bring help she talked quietly to the intruder for a few minutes. Reports differ as to what happened next. Not in dispute is the fact that the bumble-footed police took fully 12 minutes to respond to the emergency.

Needless to say, the Queen was both extremely angry and deeply upset. Security had been beefed up after the death of Lord Mountbatten from an IRA bomb three years earlier, yet incredibly it could still allow a stranger to climb through a window and bail up the Queen in her own bed.

But the break-in was not the only alarming event to take place in a year already darkened by worry over the Falklands War in which Prince Andrew had served as a helicopter pilot. On 20 July as a detachment of the Blues and Royals approached Horse Guards Parade from Hyde Park, an IRA car bomb exploded, killing four guardsmen and injuring 17 spectators. Two hours later a second bomb in Regents Park killed seven more of the Queen's men and injured a further 24.

The scale and callousness of the attack, and its proximity to Buckingham Palace, shocked the country. This latest atrocity renewed fears that the Queen herself could be on the hit list.

LEFT: BRAVE. QUEEN ELIZABETH IS NOT immune from personal threat at public ceremonies such as the Trooping of the Colour, where in earlier years she could be seen on her favourite mount Winston (pictured). Security was increased after 1981 when six blank shots were fired at her as she rode down the Mall.

BELOW: ASSASSINATED. IN 1979 Prince Phillip's uncle, Earl Mountbatten of Burma, was blown up by Irish terrorists while he was fishing off Mullaghmore near his summer home of Cassiebawn Castle in Ireland.

While the Queen had come in for flak over the failed Windsor marriages – Charles and Diana would finally separate in December – it might be expected that the fire would have earned her considerable sympathy. But no. It prompted instead an outcry over the possibility that the British taxpayer might have to pick up the tab for repairs to the State-owned castle. (As it turned out, the Queen agreed to foot the bulk of the bill.)

So 1992 came to an end with a horrific blaze, an acrimonious marriage split and a certain amount of ill-feeling toward the Monarchy. The Queen had every reason to feel deeply depressed.

But Elizabeth is a resilient woman. And a philosophical one. In her Christmas message she described how the worries of a 'sombre year' had been put into perspective by the selfless example of close friend Leonard Cheshire VC who, even while suffering from a terminal illness, had continued to put other people first.

She added: 'If we can sometimes lift our eyes from our own problems, and focus on those of others it will be . . . a step in the right direction.'

ABOVE: INEVITABLE. THE WRITING had been on the wall all year, and finally in December came news that the Prince and Princess of Wales were to separate. Public sympathy was all with Diana, and Charles faced an uphill battle to repair his damaged reputation. People saw him as the villain of the piece, not only for his uncaring treatment of Diana, but his flagrant disregard of his marriage vows. The following year Charles attempted to put his side of the story. In a television interview he claimed that only after his marriage had 'irretrievably broken down' had he been unfaithful. Few believed him and the public admission reportedly infuriated his family.

ABOVE: PASSIONATE INTIMACY. Diana's 'Squidgy' tapes might have raised eyebrows but published details of a recorded telephone conversation between the Prince of Wales and Camilla Parker Bowles caused a furore. Not only did the 'Camillagate' tape prove conclusively that Princess Diana was justified in blaming her husband's infidelity for her marriage breakdown, but its vulgar tone – complete with the now infamous reference to tampons – seemed more appropriate to a bargain-bin paperback than the heir to the throne. How the Queen must have fumed! It turned out that the Prince had been secretly meeting his lover for more than a decade.

ABOVE: CELEBRATION. THE ONE bright spot in a dark year – Princess Anne married her long-time love, Commander Timothy Laurence. Royal reporter Ben Barclay took the opportunity of stepping boldly into the Queen's shoes and offering the Princess a word or two of advice: 'Your new husband, Tim, is a splendid young man – we all liked him so much when he was the naval equerry at the palace – but you must let him be master in his own household. That has always been the way of the Windsors. The men come first (except when one is Queen, of course), so don't boss him about so much in public.'

ABOVE: COMFORT. THE YEAR THAT HAD STARTED OFF with such promise had ended on a decidedly bleak note. But if Elizabeth was down – she certainly was not out. A Queen cannot afford to be crushed by the weight of adversity. The show must go on and as she farewelled her annus horibillis, Elizabeth revealed that she had been heartened and 'deeply touched' by the messages she had received from ordinary people who had offered her their prayers and understanding.

RIGHT: SELFLESS EXAMPLE. IN HER CHRISTMAS message the Queen described how her worries had been put into perspective by her friend Leonard Cheshire VC who, even while terminally ill, had continued to put other people first. Cheshire is seen here with his wife Sue Ryder while in New Zealand in 1979 to raise money for humanitarian work in India.

Chapter Eight

ANNUS EVEN MORE
HORRIBILIS

IN A WAY 1997 WAS AN ANNUS
HORRIBILIS MAXIMUS. NOT
FOR A SERIES OF DISASTERS
BUT BECAUSE OF ONE
MOMENTOUS EVENT – THE
DEATH OF PRINCESS DIANA.

The car crash in Paris that killed the Princess and her lover Dodi Al Fayed on 31 August shocked the world and sparked an unprecedented outpouring of grief. A sea of floral tributes piled up outside Kensington Palace and people wept in the streets.

This former *Weekly* editor found her conscience pricking. We had always tried to be fair in our coverage of Diana's marriage troubles and published reliably sourced material. Even so, in retrospect, some of the stories ('Di's Wild Spending', 'What Stress Has Done to Diana', 'Inside The Anguished Mind of a Princess') now seemed intrusive and unkind.

The Princess – so beautiful, compassionate and misunderstood – was cruelly taken just as she seemed at last to be finding some happiness. If ordinary people mourned, what must the royal family be feeling? At a time of tragedy, past differences are forgotten. Surely, they must be utterly devastated.

OPPOSITE: 'A CARPET OF FLOWERS. IT SEEMED THAT THE whole world mourned the death of Princess Diana and, as the floral tributes piled up outside Kensington Palace during the first days of September 1997, grief-stricken crowds grew angry. Where was the Queen? Why hadn't she made a public statement, given some sign that she cared? The British tabloids took up the cry. 'Your people are suffering. Speak to us Ma'am,' said the *Mirror*.

ABOVE: TWINGES OF CONSCIENCE. DETAILS OF DIANA'S marital difficulties over the past decade had provided the popular press – the *Weekly* included – with page after page of gripping reading. Now the beautiful, compassionate, misunderstood Princess was dead, and in retrospect those stories appeared intrusive and unkind.

LEFT: ATTACKED. A GRIM-FACED QUEEN ARRIVES AT Westminster Abbey for the funeral of Princess Diana on 6 September. Compounding her grief was the knowledge that, together with other senior members of the royal family, she had badly misjudged the prevailing mood. By failing to share her feelings openly with a sorrowing nation, she had made the monarchy vulnerable to attack.

The world waited for a heartfelt message from the Queen, a lowered flag at Buckingham Palace, tears in royal eyes, some sign that she shared the public grief. Other than a news picture of a drawn-looking Elizabeth leaving a church service, none was forthcoming.

In deciding to remain in seclusion for several days at Balmoral, the Queen – or her advisors – made an error that reflected badly on the royal family and caused a storm of protest.

Nobody outside her immediate circle knows exactly what was on the Queen's mind at that terrible time. Most probably she viewed the tragedy as a private family affair. Her press secretary later said her first thought had been to support and protect the devastated young Princes. Whatever the reason, the Queen badly misjudged the prevailing mood. When she finally issued a personal statement couched in her usual measured tones and appeared in public it was too little, too late.

At Diana's funeral in Westminster Abbey, her brother Earl Spencer delivered a stinging side-swipe at Buckingham Palace. '[Diana] would want us today to pledge ourselves to protecting her beloved boys, William and Harry . . . and I do this here, Diana, on your behalf,' he said. 'We will not allow them to suffer the anguish that used regularly to drive you to tearful despair. I pledge that we, your blood family, will do all we can to continue the imaginative, loving way in which you were steering these two exceptional young men, so that their souls are not simply immersed by duty and tradition but can sing as openly as you planned.'

The Earl's words met with applause in the Abbey and cheers from the vast numbers listening to the broadcast service outside.

So there! That was telling them! Had the royals treated Diana as she should have been treated, and had Charles been a loving husband, there would have been no marriage breakdown and no Dodi Al Fayed. The Queen of Hearts would not then have been hounded to her death by the evil paparazzi in that Paris tunnel.

The monarchy has always had its detractors – the soap-opera events of 1992 had raised derisive jeers – but this was something else. This was real public anger.

Mourners – two million came to London for the funeral – accused the Queen and her family of being unfeeling and unsympathetic and out of touch with the spirit of the age.

LEFT: COURAGE. PRINCE Charles, with Princes William and Harry, the Duke of Edinburgh and Diana's brother Earl Spencer. Later Prince Charles would pay tribute to his sons. 'I am unbelievably proud of William and Harry,' he said. 'They are really quite remarkable. I think they have handled an extraordinary time with quite enormous courage and the greatest possible dignity.'

LEFT: HALF-MAST AT LAST. PEOPLE expected to see a flag flying at half-mast above Buckingham Palace. Yet, while every public building across the country flew a lowered national flag as a mark of respect to Diana, the palace flagpole remained stubbornly bare. It turned out that the Queen, who had remained at Balmoral, was reluctant to bend the rules. Protocol decreed that the royal standard marking the sovereign's presence must be the only flag flying at the palace; and that it could never be at half-mast as it symbolised the institution of monarchy. Surely, however, this was an exceptional circumstance! It took several days before the Queen agreed. The standard was replaced by a lowered Union Jack.

ABOVE: TEARS ON THE STREET. AND ALSO ANGER AT THE Queen and her family. A poll for Britain's *Sunday Times* conducted shortly after Diana's death found that seven out of 10 people believed that the Queen was out of touch, with more than half believing she should abdicate. British Prime Minister Tony Blair added his voice to the mood of disenchantment when he declared that the royal family must adapt or die.

ABOVE: FAREWELL. ATOP DIANA'S CASKET, CREAM LILIES and a poignant card from her sons. The *Weekly* marked the Princess's death with an issue in which staff members shared their special memories. Said Donna Fleming: 'I got to stand next to Diana [in 1983] and was awe-struck, not only because she was so stunning to look at, but because she seemed so gracious and genuine.'

Of course, Elizabeth was no stranger to criticism. She had learned early on that the deference with which both press and public then treated royalty could disappear in a flash. She got her first real taste of disapproval when she left her children, Anne just a baby, in the care of nurses and nannies in London for several months while she joined naval officer Philip in Malta. What sort of a mother, some people asked, would willingly do such a thing? The six-month 1953-54 Commonwealth tour during which the youngsters again stayed home brought similar tut-tutting. She might be Queen, but surely Elizabeth didn't have to put duty ahead of family life to that extent.

Three years later it was her speeches that came in for flak. In an unexpected 1957 outburst that led to him being labelled a 'bounder' and 'someone who ought to be shot', Lord Altrincham (the journalist and historian John Grigg who later renounced his peerage) described the Queen's 'utterances' as those of a 'priggish schoolgirl'.

Certainly Elizabeth did have a girlish speaking voice, and her cut-glass references to 'may husband and ay' became the stuff of music-hall jokes (she herself would later also see the humour). But it was the content of her speeches that really got up the young peer's nose. The Queen, he sniffed, seemed 'unable to string even a few sentences together without a written text' and thus depended on her advisors, a fuddy-duddy bunch lacking in gumption, to put words in her mouth.

If her speechmakers let her down it was felt that – in the early days, at least – her fashion advisors, who included autocratic elderly dresser Bobo MacDonald, did likewise. The Queen was a young and attractive woman. Why did she have to get about in such matronly outfits? Why couldn't she give veteran designer Norman Hartnell the push and find someone with more up-to-the-minute ideas? And surely that stiff off-the-face hairstyle could do with some modernising.

ABOVE: ABSENTEE PARENT. THE QUEEN IS NO STRANGER to criticism. She first felt the chill of disapproval while still a Princess, when she left her small children in the care of her parents and nannies in London while she joined her naval officer husband Philip in Malta.

ABOVE: PRIM AND PROPER. THE NEWLY CROWNED Queen at her desk. Elizabeth never pretended to be a fashion leader. Nevertheless, her early 'working clothes' – even by the sedate standards of the 1950s – often seemed unnecessarily stiff and staid.

LEFT: OOPS! THE DUKE OF Edinburgh is noted for his quick wit and earthy humour, but sometimes his bluntness landed him in hot water. His 'get your fingers out' instruction to employers and workers locked in bitter battles during the 1960s offended many, and a reference to 'slitty eyes' branded him the 'Great Wally of China'.

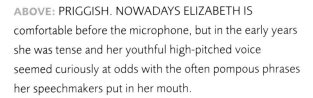

ABOVE: PRIGGISH. NOWADAYS ELIZABETH IS comfortable before the microphone, but in the early years she was tense and her youthful high-pitched voice seemed curiously at odds with the often pompous phrases her speechmakers put in her mouth.

ABOVE: MATRONLY. THE QUEEN IN NEW ZEALAND IN 1963. The Weekly might have applauded Elizabeth's fashions, but others were less enthusiastic. Fashion gurus took her designers to task for producing matronly styles unsuited to her youthful looks.

Even the royal smile – or lack of it – came in for the odd pot-shot. Elizabeth's features, in repose, could look undeniably severe (her relatives called it her 'chinless' expression and she herself would later refer to her 'Miss Piggy' look), but coupled with a natural shyness was her conviction that her demeanour should reflect the solemnity of her position. After all, her father King George VI seldom raised a smile in public and nobody criticised him.

This was fairly trivial stuff. More serious was the anger directed at the royal family's traditional delight in blood sport; in 1957 Elizabeth's expertise at reducing the deer population of Sandringham saw the League Against Cruel Sports label her as the country's worst offender.

Four years later the Queen again found herself in the gun. During a tiger shoot in India, Philip put paid to one of these magnificent animals and a photograph of the hunting party proudly standing around its corpse appeared on the front pages of newspapers around the world. While the Queen did not appear exactly delighted, she nevertheless allowed herself to be photographed with the trophy and thus became a target for the public and media indignation that followed. (Philip would go on to cause further offence – principally over foot-in-the-mouth comments such as a reference to 'slitty-eyed foreigners' for which he inspired a headline: 'The Great Wally of China'.)

ABOVE: BLOOD SPORTS. HUNTING AND SHOOTING ARE traditional pursuits of royalty. George VI took delight in dispatching creatures great and small (in a single day at Balmoral the King and his party once bagged more than a dozen different varieties of wildlife) and Elizabeth also became proficient with a rifle. In 1957 she fell foul of the League Against Cruel Sports which labelled her its royal enemy number one.

LEFT: SEVERE. ONE SIMPLY CAN'T BE EXPECTED TO SMILE all the time! King George VI seldom raised more than the faintest suggestion of a smile in public. This was deemed appropriate for it reflected the solemnity of his position. But when the Queen fails to appear joyful – as on this occasion during her 1990 visit – it is thought she must be displeased. Elizabeth calls a serious expression her Miss Piggy face.

RIGHT: STYLISH. BY 1997 FUSSY ensembles and mumsy headgear had all but disappeared from the Queen's travelling wardrobe. This simple but stylish hat won praise during the 1986 tour.

MARCH 17, 1986 90c
NEW ZEALAND
WOMAN'S
Weekly
ROYAL VISIT'86
12 EXCLUSIVE COLOUR PAGES
SOUVENIR EDITION

ABOVE: RADIANT. NOT THE SLIGHTEST hint of Miss Piggy here! Judging from the *Weekly's* 12-page coverage of the 1986 New Zealand tour the royal smile was seldom absent – even though the Queen had good cause to let it flag. We pointed out that she had not only endured egg-throwing and buttocks-baring incidents, but had undertaken some peculiar engagements – like visiting the Taupo swamp and renaming the road to the Nelson tip.

Elizabeth seemed to learn from these early brickbats. In the 40 years since the first critical onslaught her speeches became less stiff and more relevant, and her fashion sense improved out of sight. She lightened up in public to the extent of confessing that she sometimes 'simply ached with smiling' and would no more pose for the press anywhere near a shot tiger than dance a jig at the opening of Parliament.

She also became, as one commentator put it, 'sanguine' toward carping personal criticism and stoically endured the never-ending dysfunctional family and royal soap-opera jibes.

In 1997, however, she could not afford to turn her back on the public mood. Diana was dead and the Windsors were being slammed over their frozen reaction to the tragedy.

OPPOSITE: DIANA'S EXAMPLE. DIANA HAD BEEN KIND and compassionate, and had reached out to people. Writers warned that unless the royal family learned to unbend and show their human side the monarchy could face 'the final chapter in the royal fairytale'.

FASHION CRITICS SILENCED

In 1977 Ian Thomas, one of three designers with a Royal Warrant, hit back at fashion writers who wanted to see the Queen 'looking like a model from one of the glossies'.

'She has to wear her clothes – walk about, sit down, stand up, shake hands, get in and out of cars,' he pointed out. 'They're real working clothes and they have to look as good at the end of a function as at the beginning.'

Even so, they could still be stylish and whether due to his influence or not (Thomas accomplished a breakthrough when he put her in culottes), by 1997 the Queen's 'working clothes' had become distinctly more so.

And her fashion critics had fallen silent.

While still designed along classical lines, in terms of colour the Queen had become a real trend-setter. At a time of life when many of her contemporaries opted for subdued elderly lady hues, the 70-plus Elizabeth regularly made a splash in peacock blue, red, lime green, and even canary yellow.

ABOVE: THE QUEEN IN CULOTTES? An artist's impression of trendy leisure-wear outfits designed for the Queen in the late 1970s.

LEFT: BOLD. THE 1980S AND 90S saw Elizabeth stepping out in ever more colourful outfits. She is pictured here in Buckle Street, Wellington, in 1986.

Woman's Weekly

...nd farewell
to ...ur darling
Q...en Mum

NZ *Woman's* **WEEKLY**

EXCLUSIVE
Your pet can
be a star!

NZ SHAME
Why more kids
are home alone

Golden Wedding Tribute

**QUEEN ELIZABETH's
lasting love secrets**

WIN! Escape with your family to Surfer's Paradise p 77

Chapter Nine

OUR GRACIOUS QUEEN

THE QUEEN'S GOLDEN JUBILEE YEAR – AND SUDDENLY SHE WAS TOP OF THE POPS. AT VARIOUS VENUES AROUND BRITAIN IN 2002 VAST CROWDS TURNED OUT TO HONOUR THE WOMAN WHO ONLY FIVE YEARS EARLIER HAD BEEN ANGRILY LABELLED AS UNFEELING, UNBENDING, OUT OF TOUCH AND PAST HER USE-BY DATE.

What had happened to bring about such a dramatic change of heart? First, the hysteria surrounding Diana's death which had sparked clarion calls for modernisation of the monarchy – Prime Minister Tony Blair declared that the royal family must adapt or die – had long since died down.

But its lesson had been heeded. The public had asked for a show of emotion. They had wanted to see the royals' human side. They had wanted the Queen and her family to be more approachable. And while there had been no dramatic relaxation of formality, the Queen had shown that, as she put it, she was 'trying hard' to read the public message.

Who would have thought, for instance, that they would ever see Elizabeth in a pub, even if it was only for seven minutes? Or photographed in front of McDonalds?

Second, Diana's death had left a giant blank in reporters' notebooks. With the star of the show out of the picture, the popular press turned its attention to other family members. Whereas the younger royals' misdemeanours continued to provide

tittle-tattle, Charles's evident success at forging a closer relationship with his two boys – for he now had to be both mother and father to William and Harry – gained increasing approval, and the sedate activities of Elizabeth II which Diana once would have pushed off tabloid front pages got more of a look-in.

ABOVE: NOT A FILM STAR. IN APRIL 1986 THE *WEEKLY* celebrated the Queen's 60th birthday with a special feature by royal correspondent Raymond Fullager. He defended Elizabeth's formal approach: 'On the big occasions she has always tended to wear rather wooden expressions . . . But as Head of State, constitutional monarch and Head of the Church of England, she cannot allow herself to relax, smile or joke in public like ordinary people . . . She is the antithesis of the Hollywood film star. She doesn't show off. She won't perform.'

OPPOSITE: SUBTLE CHANGE. IN RECENT YEARS the Queen – seen here in New Zealand – has gradually become more relaxed in public. Yet during the hysteria of September 1997, people demanded that Elizabeth loosen up still further. She did. But only so much. It would have been ludicrous to expect a woman in her 70s suddenly to become all touchy-feely like Diana.

The jubilee year saw the sympathy vote going the Queen's way. How cruel that the fates should have picked on this, of all times, to strike two such heavy blows. First Princess Margaret succumbed to a series of strokes. Then the world's beloved Queen Mum died. The loss of the Queen Mother, coming so close after Princess Margaret's death, hit the Queen particularly hard. Elizabeth had been exceptionally close to her mother. The Queen Mum had been her rock. The indomitable old lady had seemed somehow indestructible. Now her daughter provided the public with something they had wanted to see five years ago – a glimpse of the private person. A glimpse of vulnerability.

Royal correspondent James Whittaker wrote: 'When Diana died [the Queen] spoke kind, comforting words out of a sense of duty and respect. But when her mother died it was all about love. The Queen opened her heart in a way we have not seen before.'

Again, it was just a small thing, but enough. Fundamentally, Elizabeth was never going to change. And nor should she. It would have been ludicrous to expect a woman in her 70s, famous for her dignified reserve, suddenly to become all touchy-feely like Diana.

ABOVE: MUCH LOVED. SHE WAS 101 YEARS OLD AND everyone knew that the end could not be far away. Nevertheless, when the ailing Queen Mother died shortly after watching her younger daughter laid to rest it left an emptiness – and not just for the Queen and other members of the royal family. Britain and the Commonwealth mourned the passing of a woman of great charm who had become a beacon of majesty, decency and permanence in an increasingly violent world.

ABOVE: GRIEF. PRINCESS MARGARET'S DEATH WAS THE first of two devastating losses suffered by the Queen in 2002. For many years Margaret had suffered from complaints thought to be related to heavy smoking and drinking. The Princess – pictured at the Chelsea Flower Show in 2000 – succumbed to a series of strokes.

ABOVE: POPULAR. THE QUEEN IS GREETED BY BRITISH Prime Minister Tony Blair as she arrives for an official dinner to mark the start of her 50th jubilee celebrations. Five years earlier the British press had given her a right royal roasting. Now all that had been forgotten, and Elizabeth was top of the pops.

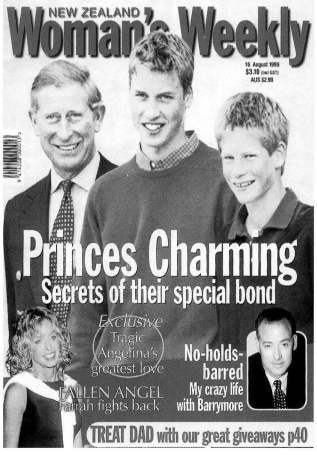

NEW ZEALAND

Woman's Weekly

16 August 1999
$3.10 (incl GST)
AUS $2.90

Princes Charming
Secrets of their special bond

Exclusive
Tragic
Angelina's
greatest love

FALLEN ANGEL
Farrah fights back

No-holds-barred
My crazy life
with Barrymore

TREAT DAD with our great giveaways p40

ABOVE: AFFECTION. NEW ZEALAND HAS NEVER subjected the Queen to the kind of criticism she has endured at home. Nevertheless, Kiwi crowds that turn out to greet her have dwindled in recent years. Blind devotion is a thing of the past and royalty is no longer held in awe. The undignified behaviour of younger family members has seen to that. However, the Queen's unwavering dedication to duty continues to earn affection and respect and, as this picture from her 1990 tour shows, a glimpse of the sovereign in person is still cause for excitement.

LEFT: CLOSE RELATIONSHIP. AFTER PRINCESS DIANA'S death Charles pulled out all the stops in his effort to be the best possible solo dad to sons William and Harry. And they, in their turn, helped him shed some of his stiff public image. Said Harold Brooks-Baker, editor of *Burke's Peerage:* 'The House of Windsor didn't really move into a natural way of doing things until the death of the Princess of Wales. What's happening now is part of her legacy . . . The boys are acting in the same way as young people today from all classes – they bring their parents up to speed with the latest trends and the modern world.'

But there was another, more significant reason. And the royal hairdressers provided a clue.

People have sometimes wondered why the Queen has never varied her hairstyle. According to royal biographer Ann Morrow, it is because she wishes to present the same face to the world – an image of stability and continuity. And in the fear and feelings of insecurity that followed the horror of the September 11 terrorist attack on the twin towers in New York, never was stability and a sense of continuity more desperately needed.

Synonymous with those qualities was resilience – something that the Queen had shown in abundance. For the family dramas had kept on coming. In 2001 Sophie Wessex became the victim of a sting by an undercover reporter, posing as an Arab sheikh, to whom she bad-mouthed the royal family. Prince Harry's experiments with marijuana earned him the dubious tag of Harry Pothead, and Princess Anne's daughter Zara Phillips gave the press a field day when she engaged in an unseemly public brawl with jockey boyfriend Richard Johnson after an evening spent at a pub.

LEFT AND BELOW: THEN AND NOW. Nearly 40 years separate these two pictures. The Queen's hair has greyed but the style remains the same. Admittedly, Elizabeth's coiffeur is restricted both by its suitability for hats and tiaras and by the need for people to see her features clearly. (A fringe or floaty tendrils would never do.) But there is a more significant reason for the changeless look. The Queen wishes to present the same face to the world. In our increasingly troubled and insecure times, she sees herself as symbolising stability and a sense of continuity.

ABOVE RIGHT: REBELLIOUS. LIKE MANY OTHER teenagers, Prince Harry liked to push the boundaries. But laddish Harry was not just any teenager. When the drunken Prince vomited across the bar at the Duke of Grosvenor's home and smoked cannabis behind a store shed at the back of the Rattlebone Pub, all Britain soon heard about it. A 'shock' visit to a drug rehabilitation centre reportedly prompted Harry to mend his ways.

LEFT: EMBARRASSING lapse. Sophie, the Countess of Wessex, seemed such a sensible person, even a bit dull. Surely she could never become tabloid fodder. But she did. In April 2001, the naive PR consultant made indiscreet remarks about members of the royal family to a newspaper reporter posing as an Arab sheikh. Not surprisingly, they cost her her job. She has since become a full-time working royal.

TOP LEFT AND ABOVE: TEMPESTUOUS. Zara Phillips in Auckland where she attended the Sportsperson of the Century Awards in February 2000. Princess Anne's headstrong daughter was the model of decorum in New Zealand but later gave the press a field day when she engaged in a public punching, kicking and screaming match with boyfriend Richard Johnson. The stormy relationship finally ended in 2002.

In the wake of books by biographers not noted for their affection toward Princess Diana (Lady Colin Campbell claimed that the Princess had aborted the love child of art dealer Oliver Hoare, and Penny Junor alleged that she had made telephone death threats to Camilla Parker Bowles), a third arrived by a so-called friend. Former Royal Protection Squad officer Ken Wharfe painted 'the People's Princess' as a raunchy young woman who kept a vibrator in her handbag. Speculation about red-haired Harry's resemblance to Diana's lover James Hewitt rumbled on. The 'love rat' himself blabbed about the affair, claiming that Charles had known about it all along; and intimate letters written to him by Diana were offered to one of the tabloids.

While Charles's relationship with 'the love of his life' Camilla had gained increasing public acceptance, future prospects for the middle-aged lovers continued to fascinate. Was the Queen coming round to accepting Camilla? Would the two ever be able to marry? Commentators warned of constitutional headaches ahead.

It would have been too much to expect that the jubilee year might pass without a major scandal. And sure enough there were revelations of sleazy goings-on in Charles's household. But it was the aborted trial of Princess Diana's former butler Paul Burrell on charges of theft of some of the Princess's belongings that hit closest to home. Was it fear of unflattering things Burrell might reveal about the royals that caused the Queen suddenly to remember a conversation she'd had with Burrell that effectively exonerated him? Or was it a tardy resolve to let compassion take precedence over protocol? Regardless of the answer, one thing seems clear. Elizabeth will never be far away from controversy.

So how does a woman in her mid-70s, at a time of life when slippers and feet up are the lot of many, continue to cope with the unrelenting pressure of public expectation, not to mention the sheer physical demands of her work schedule? What is the secret of that amazing resilience?

On the physical side, the Queen must be thankful that she has inherited her mother's sturdy constitution which includes 'good Scottish legs'. (She once revealed that the secret of standing comfortably for hours was to 'keep one's feet apart

ABOVE: ACCEPTANCE. ONCE HER NAME WAS MUD – shoppers threw bread rolls at her in the supermarket – so it wasn't surprising that after Diana's death Camilla Parker Bowles went to ground. But over the past few years, she has gradually 'come out'. Helped by a style makeover designed to enhance her suitability as a companion for Charles, Camilla has won a degree of public approval.

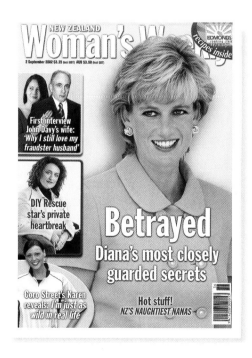

ABOVE: FALSE FRIEND. PRINCESS DIANA ONCE regarded police bodyguard Ken Wharfe as a friend to whom she could unload her secrets. In 2002 Wharf repaid the privilege with a tell-all book in which he portrayed the Princess as a raunchy woman who kept a vibrator in her handbag.

LEFT: COLLAPSE. DIANA'S former butler Paul Burrell leaves Bow Street magistrate's court in central London after denying that he had stolen hundreds of the Princess's possessions. Part-way through the trial the Queen 'suddenly' remembered that he had told her of removing Diana's things for safekeeping. The information exonerated him and the trial collapsed. Burrell later put the knife into the Spencer family, accusing Earl Spencer of hypocrisy, Diana's sister Lady Sarah McCorquodale of initially wanting to bag Charles for herself, and the Princess's angry mother Frances Shand Kydd of 'using the kind of language you would never expect a mother ever to say to a daughter'.

RIGHT: STRONG SCOTTISH LEGS. Queen Mary once famously declared: 'We are royal – we never get tired and we never get ill.' Her granddaughter Elizabeth must be grateful that she has inherited Mary's good health and indomitable will. From the Queen Mother comes another important asset – strong Scottish legs. The Queen is seen here in 1970 at Eden Park, Auckland, chatting to Prime Minister Keith Holyoake. Princess Anne (also displaying a splendid pair of legs) stands nearby with Auckland Mayor Sir Dove-Myer Robinson.

THE OFF-DUTY QUEEN

She enjoys enormous privilege and wealth, yet the Queen is basically a woman of simple tastes whose heart lies firmly in the countryside.

Biographers paint a picture of the off-duty Queen as seldom happier than when dressed in headscarf and sturdy shoes tramping among the heathers of her estate at Balmoral or at Sandringham with dogs at heel. Apparently, guests at Balmoral used to dread an invitation to walk with their hostess, for she set such a brisk pace that she soon had them puffing.

Rich food gets the royal thumbs-down. A favourite is simple shepherd's pie (but with creamed leeks on top), and if alone the Queen may settle for scrambled eggs for supper. Unlike the Queen Mum, who was an enthusiastic devotee of gin and tonic, she goes easy on the alcohol, usually preferring plain Malvern mineral water, although dry Martini is currently said to be a favourite Christmas stiffener.

Elizabeth's frugality with alcohol extends to other areas. She is renowned among other members of her family for her hatred of extravagance and waste. Sources say she really does go around switching off lights, and she has also been known to check the contents of fridges to see what is left over and inquire what is to be done with it.

While the on-duty Queen sometimes appears solemn, the informal sovereign has a delicious sense of fun, is a marvellous mimic and participates enthusiastically in after-dinner parlour games during family get-togethers.

She also has a ready wit. The story is told of the occasion when, while driving to Balmoral, Elizabeth spotted an interesting-looking little shop and popped in to investigate.

'You look awfully like the Queen,' said the shopkeeper.

'How very reassuring,' she replied.

ABOVE: SLIM, TRIM AND HEALTHY. IF ELIZABETH POLISHED off everything placed before her during official dinners, she'd have been Queen Blobby years ago. But the Queen, who in her childhood and teenage years was surrounded by candies, scones, pies and Yorkshire puddings (and became somewhat chubby as a result) uses her formidable willpower to resist temptation. She tastes only a little of what she is offered and goes easy on the alcohol.

LEFT: A COUNTRYWOMAN AT HEART. ELIZABETH IS seldom happier than when following country pursuits. She is an accomplished horsewoman and, like her late mother, a keen race-goer. While noted for her love of corgis, the Queen also breeds labradors, and trudging across the countryside with several great wet dogs is her idea of heaven.

. . . and make sure the weight is evenly distributed'.) Apart from odd bouts of sinusitis for which she takes homeopathic remedies she is generally untroubled by illness.

In times of difficulty and stress, Elizabeth knows she can count on Philip to be there for her. The relationship between the Queen and her husband is described as that of loving friends who have been through a lot together and supported each other every step of the way.

The Queen also draws strength from the many kind messages she receives. In her 'annus horribilis' Christmas speech she took pains to thank ordinary people – many with troubles of their own – who had offered their 'prayers, understanding and sympathy'. As well, she is sustained by a deep personal faith.

She said last Christmas: 'I know that the only way to live is to try to do what is right, to take the long view, to give of my best in all that the day brings and to put my trust in God.'

In a broadcast to mark her 21st birthday the then Princess Elizabeth made a solemn promise to her future subjects. 'I declare before you,' she said, 'that my whole life, whether it be long or short, shall be devoted to your service . . . '

And at the 50th anniversary of her coronation, the Queen can take pride in the fact that, through good times and bad, she has never wavered on that vow.

Images appearing in this book are, in the main, the property of New Zealand Magazines and have been drawn from the New Zealand Magazines photo archive. Other images are acknowledged below. New Zealand Magazines also thanks Her Majesty Queen Elizabeth II for permission to use material through The Royal Collection. Special thanks to Simon Iles and Reuters for permission to use the Reuters photographs included in this book. Efforts have been made to confirm the copyright holders of all photographs. In a few instances this has not been possible and the publisher would be pleased to hear from these copyright holders.

Abbreviations: t = top, m = middle, b = base, l = left, c = centre, r = right.

Crown copyright reserved: pp. 6br, copyright Raphael Tucker and Sons Ltd, England. Original painting by James Gunn, now in Belgian Institute, London; 7, Cecil Beaton; 8br, The Royal Collection © 2003, Her Majesty Queen Elizabeth II; 8tr, 8bl, 9, 12r, 14bl, 21br, 22r.

Reuters: pp. 26, 62br, 63t, 80bc, 81br, 82l, 83br, 90l, 96t, 104bl, 104br, 107tr, 109t.

TRANZ: pp. 20l, 23tl, 55l, 55br, 59br, 61t, 60m, 70, 71t, 71b, 75b, 78b.

Other: pp. 11t, British Tourist Authority; 14tl, Royal Geographical Society; 18mr, International News Photos; 22r and 47bl, Studio Lisa; 79, ONF; 87br, Robin Morrison estate/ Dinah Morrison, *New Zealand Listener.*